I have wanted to write this book since 1985. As a six-year-old girl I had no idea that selective mutism even existed, but my silence was palpable, and inside of it I was developing all kinds of conversations, explanations, questions, and insights.

I didn't have the words back then to explain the way I was feeling, and even if I did, I found it extremely difficult to share what was going on for me with anyone, even my parents. I felt challenged because people talked about my choice to not speak and asked me about it a lot … but no matter how I tried, I couldn't answer their questions.

I had no way of telling people that my silence was not a choice. I had things I wanted to say, but I couldn't physically say them. I longed to answer their questions. I had many questions of my own too, but all those words remained stuck inside of me, where they have simmered and developed for many years.

I found out about selective mutism when I was thirty years old, and straightaway hundreds of memories from my past started to make sense. It felt as though I had suddenly learned what the numbers were for on a very complicated 'connect the dots' puzzle. I was reminded of my six-year-old desire to help people to understand, and since then I have been joining dots.

My opinion is that, along with the potential for selective mutism, comes many wonderful traits and talents that need to be celebrated. People like me are usually sensitive, intelligent, creative, intuitive, imaginative, observant, capable, and so much more. Whether you, your child, or someone else you know suffers from selective mutism, I hope this book will help you to face the challenges and embrace the goodness that they hold.

There is little

in my life that

brings me more joy

than the ability to

connect with and

speak my own words.

I HAVE SOMETHING TO SAY!

AN EXPLORATION INTO THE HEART AND MIND OF MY SELECTIVE MUTISM

KATHRYN HARPER

This paperback edition first published in 2015 by

Green Cup Publishing

Wanaka, New Zealand

www.greencuppublishing.com

ISBN#: 978-0-473-32816-0

- For Mum –

I know you would have loved this book
when I was small xx

I believe that the challenges
we face in our lives are
there for a reason.
I think of them as directions,
showing us the **best and most
fulfilling ways to grow**.

About this book

My name is Kathryn Harper and I have written this book based upon my experiences with selective mutism. As you read it you will learn that I suffered from selective mutism as a child, and developed further complications from my unmanaged anxiety in my teens and early adult years. Today I am a 36-year-old mum of two. Since having my children I have gained a much more expanded perspective about my life, and I have been able to connect back to my childhood desire to share as openly as I can.

My intention is to tell you my story, with the overall aim of helping people who find themselves in similar situations to realize that they are not alone – and hopefully to gain some comfort from this fact. One of the most difficult things for me to try to come to terms with as I grew up was the fact that I felt alone in my feelings. I found it extremely difficult to express myself, and longed to know that this didn't make me weird, abnormal or wrong. I wanted to know that I had a place in the world and that I could make a difference.

Through the book I share both my past and present perspectives, and go into lessons learned and insights gained. In some sections I add a few words of advice. I'd like to point out here that, in my opinion, there are many ways to any destination – and so please take what you like and leave out what you don't. I don't assume to know anything about your own unique experience, and so your experience of selective mutism may differ from mine.

Most of all, I wish to encourage you to read this book with an open heart. I hope that, whatever your connection to selective mutism, you enjoy reading my words and upon closing these pages I leave you with a little more peace and a little less pain.

Contents

People with selective mutism find it **impossible to speak in certain situations**. In these situations, the anxiety felt is so great that it literally **freezes the vocal chords**. It is an easily misunderstood condition, so please understand that selective mutism is not a choice, and those who suffer are usually trying the best they can to communicate ...

Introduction –
What might have been ...

F*rom time to time I find myself in a strange kind of daydream. I imagine what it might be like if I were to* wake up one morning and find that the past thirty years had been a dream.

A six-year-old me would wake up, and I sometimes wonder how she would feel. What choices would she make that I didn't make when I was small? How would she see her world, knowing all that she now knows?

Would she embrace her differences, her vulnerabilities and her insecurities, her talents and her wisdom? Would she harness all that she has and then feel strong in her own sense of self? Would she find a natural route to the words she holds inside?

Would she still find it necessary to fit in – or would she find satisfaction and fulfillment in standing out as being a little different than the norm, but always entirely herself?

I guess it's easy to look back and to judge yourself and the actions (or inactions) you took back then. It's easy to wish your decisions had been different and that you had found a way to appreciate all that you had to offer despite the fact that so many people pointed out the one thing you weren't doing. It's easy to look back and figure out the different choices you might have made if you could return and fill those smaller shoes you once wore.

It's so easy to find yourself swirling in a world of regret and longing for what might have been. It's so easy to start telling yourself, "If only I'd known!"

The things I might tell people, the answers I might provide, the communication I might manage, the worries I might put to rest.

The thing is, back then ... I didn't know. I did the best that I could with all that I knew – and so did everyone around me. If they had known better, they would have behaved differently, asked different questions, tried different approaches. None of us could possibly have chosen differently because none of us knew back then what we know today.

In truth, going by the life I am leading today, there is not one thing I would actually change about my past. Today I am a thirty-six year-old mum of two. I have an incredible family. I live in a beautiful place. I work for myself; writing, drawing, and speaking my truth, and I love every ounce of it. I still wrestle with self-doubt and many long-held insecurities. Anxiety makes its appearance often, and from time to time, I still find it impossible to utter a sound.

I'm not sure if it has become easier to deal with my feelings, or perhaps it's simply that I've spent so long trying to run from them that I now find myself with no choice but to find out what they are trying to tell me. In every bubble of emotion I can appreciate that there is something for me to learn. In every flutter of my stomach, every tightening of my chest, and every tear that runs down my cheeks there is a story. A lesson. An opportunity for growth.

I feel myself expanding every day as my clarity, understanding, and sense of purpose becomes greater. I connect more deeply with the sensitive nature of my soul, and I find new ways of expressing the beauty that I have kept hidden away for so long.

Communication tumbles out of me in more and more ways as I reconnect with myself and find that not only was I made to speak with words, but I was made to speak through my actions, my creations, my impulses, and more. As I open up to communicating in different ways, I find that more of my words flow too, and with each attempt they become more authentic and resonant in their expression. I was born to say so many things in so many different ways – but many of these things have had to be patient, as I have come to realize that I can only speak my truth when I feel safe enough to do so.

In the first part of this book, I would like to share my story with you. I will share selective mutism from my perspective, the perspective of someone who has (and sometimes still does) suffer. I will explain some of the difficulties I faced when I found myself paralysed by anxiety, and unable to speak at all in certain situations.

I was a little girl whose greatest strengths were somehow lost behind the sought-after virtues of speech and a willingness to give things a go. I was a sensitive child who thought and felt deeply, who longed for solitude and silence, whose temperament didn't seem to fit with the way society was set up, and whose many talents were often pushed aside in favour of determining why I didn't talk as much as everybody else.

I believe people with a temperament like mine have a huge amount to offer the world. We have a gentle, beautiful nature, but we struggle to stay centred in the speed and exuberance of this time.

Anxiety can easily take hold, and when it does, selective mutism may present. People like me need to step back from the fast-paced, highly stimulating surroundings we are plunged into, and instead ease ourselves in gently.

I grew up thinking that there was something wrong with me, and I spent a lot of my time thinking about what that could be and how I might be fixed. When I learned about selective mutism, I realized that was my problem and that my anxiety needed to be fixed.

Over time, I began to question this 'fixing' approach. What is it about us that we need to fix? What are we really trying to achieve? What is this elusive "normal" that we hope to consider ourselves within the realms of? Is that really who we are here to be?

Over the years I have asked a lot of questions inside of my head, and I am sure that within the tangle of thoughts that constantly bombard me, I can find some answers.

Part two of this book looks beyond our personal stories and encourages us to embrace our true nature, no matter how unconventional it may be. I believe we all have wonderful qualities to offer and amazing gifts to give. We cannot find these if we are struggling to fit into an ideal that is not our own.

I don't believe I am here to strive toward the goals that my teachers once held for me. I don't believe I am here to dissolve into society the way it was when I found it.

In my opinion, society is unbalanced, and sways in favour of the talkative, confident, extrovert ideal. Others have come before me - speaking and writing about the often over-looked qualities of us quieter personalities, but I want to add my voice into the mix.

I grew up overshadowed by selective mutism, questioned about my perceived quietness with the unwavering assumption that it was a problem, and it needed to change.

My question is simply, why?

Why work to change the gentle nature of someone who is creative, intuitive, and beautiful in her own way?

Why try to fit her into a world that she was not made to fit? Why not listen to her wordless expressions and in doing so, why not allow her to expand the rest of the world and the way it works?

Pressure from both outside and then inside of me resulted in me becoming a grown woman whom I neither knew nor understood. In my early twenties I was emotionally unstable, reliant on alcohol and desperate to please. I appeared to be friendly and confident, but inside I was screaming. I went through bouts of depression, and I awoke each morning immersed in guilt and shame. I wanted, more than anything, to be myself, but I was terrified of the way I might be received. My life was not my own – I was a person who tried to fit into an imagined world that had no place for me.

This book is specifically about my experience with selective mutism – how I appeared to overcome it; the way it morphed into other issues, and how I have since worked backwards to embrace my true nature despite its previous negative associations. I have dug deep, and I have found that the only way for me to live my life is to embrace all that I am. The unseen qualities that became buried behind my selective mutism symptoms are something that I would like to bring to light. They are the reason for this book; my motivation for digging around in a past that pained me so much that I didn't like to remember much of it.

My sensitivity means that apparently small or insignificant things are likely to have quite an impact upon me. I feel deeply, and logic has no place in helping me to gain back my equilibrium. I realize today that my reactions to insignificant events such as losing a sock are in fact allowing past misunderstandings to heal. Allowing myself to feel every emotion, no matter how misplaced it might appear, has been a major factor in healing my past.

I hope, as you read my story, you can look past the details and notice how my message might apply to you, in your life. Whether you suffer from selective mutism, or someone you know does, or whether you have had a different experience of life entirely, it is all valid. I hope you enjoy and benefit from my wonderful realisation that "I have something to say!"

Part One

My Selective Mutism Story

The who, what, where, why, when of my selective mutism and some of the insights I have gained along the way ...

> *"Listen with your eyes,*
> *Listen with your eyes,*
> *And sing everything you see*
> *... "*
>
> The Rainbow Song

When I think about this song, I love its instruction to **'listen with your eyes'**. *It reminds me that communication is so much more than the words we use.*

1 – Listen with your eyes!

Communication is so much more than the words we use!

When I was two years old, I didn't know the difference between talking with my words and talking with my body. When I listened to other people speak, words were a very small part of what I noticed.

People spoke to me with their faces, gestures, feelings, thoughts, and intentions. Their expressions spoke volumes - and so did the way in which their bodies moved. I sensed the way they were feeling and could hear it in their tone of voice and the way that they spoke. I could see it in the clarity of their eyes and the fullness of each expression. I noticed what they were holding back and when they felt free enough to share themselves fully. I listened with all of my senses – and I noticed everything, whether subtle, hidden, or obvious.

Communication was rich, varied, and endless. It happened all the time in all kinds of ways.

The words a person speaks might tell a story, but the way they speak those words expands on that story in amazing ways, and then the words that remain unspoken often say even more. Suddenly the listener might sense a deeper truth within that story, or a deeper connection to the storyteller. A person's reasons for listening are not necessarily connected to the words they hear, but more because of the energy that the person speaking is able to share.

When we were children, we were all much more finely attuned to the subtle forms of communication that come before words. As a two-year-old, it therefore didn't mean a lot to me if I found it difficult to speak in certain situations. I would simply continue speaking in all those other ways. I used my body, my creativity, my face, and my actions. If those forms of communication were also too difficult, I'd expand my thoughts, feelings, and desires so another might pick up on them, and I always listened to other people in the same way.

Words, to me, are just the top layer of something that happens on so, so many levels.

When I was a baby I settled easily. I enjoyed playing by myself, and I've been told that I slept through the night from three weeks old(!) Come morning, I would wake up and play - or look around, making happy sounds at my cot and toys until someone came to pick me up.

As I grew a little older, my parents described me as having never-ending patience … I would spend hours working on a jigsaw puzzle by myself from a young age, and I loved to sit and draw or make things too.

I've always loved to spend time alone – it is something that I still crave, a time to nurture myself on a deep level where there is nothing to prove, no one to please,
just me being me.

When I turned two years old, there were a lot of changes made to my young life. It was early 1981, and the recession had hit. Alongside the birth of my younger brother, my parents made some big decisions … and so it was that, when my brother turned four months old, we all boarded a plane to South Africa, where we would spend the next three years.

I can imagine that stress levels were high as we landed in this strange country and made our flat on the thirty-second floor of Ponte, Johannesburg, our new home.

My brother, I've been told, wasn't the settled

baby that I was. My mum was twenty-six, sleep-deprived, and a stranger to the big city of Johannesburg. My dad worked long days in his new job. My brother cried and cried. And I, by all accounts, played happily by myself.

In our first six months in South Africa, we moved house five times. I don't know when it was noticed that I wasn't talking very much, but I can now understand how it might have happened.

Perhaps it was because of all the times we moved house; it has been suggested that because every time we moved house I would have to meet new children and make new friends ... eventually I stopped trying.

It may have been more to do with the upheaval and insecurity that accompanied these moves - the not knowing how long we might stay in a place and not having a permanent base that felt safe.

Maybe it was the observation of stress and anxiety that my parents were experiencing as they encountered financial difficulties and made the decision to move away for three years.

Or it might have been the addition of my younger brother to our family and the inevitable decline of attention I would have received.

It's also possible that the new (to me) culture in South Africa, including their apartheid system of racial segregation, played its part.

I can only imagine how it must have been for my parents when they realized that I didn't talk to anyone outside of our family home. Selective mutism is a little-known and little-understood condition today, but in the early 1980s it was even less so.

> *As a family we went to therapy. I saw a play therapist while my parents were interviewed to try and determine what was happening for me. They have told me that they were pretty much asked a lot of questions which seemed to be checking for the possibility of abuse. When the therapists were happy that this was not the case, they diagnosed me with 'voluntary mutism', and that was as much as they could give.*
>
> *My parents and I were given no resources or advice on dealing with the condition, and shortly after that we returned to England.*

I find it incredible to consider the idea of this approach, and as a parent myself I can only imagine the challenges faced by my parents and the thousands of others in similar situations.

In the '80s, it was believed that children like me were choosing not to speak in certain situations. Sometimes we were perceived as shy. Other times we were defiant, difficult, rude … The fact that we were clearly able to speak fluently in some places ruled out problems with our speech. I don't know if the idea that it was anxiety closing off our capabilities to communicate was even considered.

Thirty years later, we are blessed with a plethora of information available at our fingertips. You only have to type in two words to learn that selective mutism is an anxiety disorder, where the sufferer is incapable of speech in certain situations. Despite this, I am shocked to hear from many sources that selective mutism is still widely unknown and misunderstood.

Many people still believe that children who suffer are choosing to hold back their voice. Some people seem to think that people like me are trying to manipulate others or gain attention. Other people have their own explanations ...

> *I have been told that it didn't seem to bother the other kids that I didn't talk when I went to my preschool – or even when I started school ... my friends and I would play happily together, and at that young age we didn't really seem to need words.*
>
> *At a friend's sixth birthday party I was introduced as,*
>
> *"This is Kathryn. She doesn't talk because she's from Africa!"*
>
> *My parents knew that this wasn't the case, but although I had received a diagnosis it really didn't shed any light on my difficulties regarding talking.*
>
> *It was a case of feeling our way through it ... my parents had no idea what to do to help, and they were very much on their own with it. All they could do was the best they could manage – and together we fumbled through in the dark.*

2. My Comfort Zone

We all need to have a happy place ...

My Mum has described me as having had two very distinctly different personas when I was small. Firstly there was my home personality. At home with my family I was a chatty, bubbly child who was happy, relaxed and enjoyed life. Then there was my away-from-home personality, where I wasn't.

When I was young, my home and my family were my comfortable places. It was here that I could relax and be myself – smiley, happy, talkative and creative ... all those things that I couldn't be when anxiety took hold. I loved to be able to share my thoughts and talk about the things I was excited about, to laugh when things were funny and to smile when I was enjoying myself. These are really simple things – things that most people take for granted, and I probably did too - until I became aware of how difficult it was to do these things outside of my home.

When I first started school, I wore a silent mask. My anxiety was present in the tense way I held my body, my lack of facial expressions and of course the difficulty I had around speaking. There was one girl in my class whom I felt a little more comfortable around, and I could whisper to when I needed to say something.

Mum asked me what was special about this girl ... why was it that I could speak to her, but I couldn't speak to anybody else?

To me, the answer was really obvious,

"Because she's been to my house!"

An interesting thing about selective mutism is that it works around a set of conditions that appear (to me) to be set within our subconscious minds. I didn't consciously choose not to speak to anybody who hadn't been to my house, but I knew when I was six years old that my house was the catalyst that represented this particular level of comfort for me. These rules are very likely to be different for everybody – and probably change as we grow and our circumstances become different.

Immediately Mum got to work, inviting more and more children from my class around to play. Little by little my confidence grew. I became aware that there were more people who had heard my voice at school, and although I was still described as incredibly quiet, and my voice was barely audible, I was able to speak a little.

When I was at home one of my favourite things to do was to create shows and plays to put on for my parents (and also sometimes my friend's parents too). I remember putting on magic shows, pantomimes, nativity plays and circuses. I loved writing the scripts, creating the sets and the costumes, and practicing my acts. I also enjoyed making things to sell, and would set up stalls outside of my house. Everything creative was fun for me and hugely motivating.

When I look back, I can see that this creativity has always been my happy place, even when I became more withdrawn at home. It is an ease of being that knows no inhibitions, and simply flows from one moment to the next. In these moments, it doesn't matter if I am talking or not, and it doesn't matter how others perceive me. I am completely happy simply being me. No matter how lost I became in the years that followed, I could always rely on creativity to help me to return to a more centred, balanced state of being. It didn't matter if I was drawing, painting, making jewellery, sewing, writing, sculpting, or whatever — the heaviness of my unspoken words, suppressed emotions and layers of anxiety would melt away in those moments.

Home was my comfort zone, but from time to time the intensity of my emotions, the pressure of a question or the difficulty in explanation created a weight that crept into more and more corners of my life.

I was always able to speak at home, but I was not always able to say everything, especially if I felt like I could not give the answer or explanation that I knew my family were hoping to hear. It was in these moments that the ability to retreat to my room and indulge in something creative became my saviour.

I think it is hugely important to encourage children with selective mutism to pursue the thing that helps them to shine, whatever that may be. Whether they love sports, dance, art, writing, or whatever - the ability to lose yourself in the joy of doing something you adore can literally make all the difference inside of a life that is otherwise difficult and scary.

3. "There's no such word as '*can't*'"

A selective mute person literally cannot speak in certain situations ...

An inability to speak in certain situations raises all sorts of questions in people.

"Why?" is perhaps the one most often asked ... it is very difficult for many people to understand the motivations of a person who can speak fluently in one setting yet is completely mute in another.

Passing it off as shyness or rudeness is easy to do – but it does nothing to help the person who is suffering. Instead, it simply eases the confusion of the person who is trying to understand. I was personally often described as shy, quiet, and occasionally defiant. These were words that I grew a very strong distaste for, and my physical reaction to hearing them gradually became so intense that it felt like someone was sticking a knife in me as they were spoken.

The problem was that I needed to feel like I was being heard. To be seen and heard is a basic human need that we all have. I needed to have my behavior validated. I needed to feel like I was understood. Being passed off as shy, quiet, or defiant may have satisfied some people's curiosity, but inside of me I was desperate to be recognized as myself. I wanted to be told that my behavior was okay. I wanted to be told that it didn't matter. I wanted to feel that there was no pressure, to know that I would be seen and heard for my strengths despite my inability to speak much of the time.

Everywhere I went, no matter how hard I tried, my quietness followed me like a shadow – piercing my experiences with its presence, always the reminder that something wasn't quite right, but nobody really knew why.

I wasn't choosing to not speak. I didn't want to come across as being shy or quiet. It hurt me to notice that some people seemed to be judging me based upon the behavior that I felt I had no control over and felt trapped inside of. I think the most damaging thing for me was the fact that I felt massively misunderstood. I couldn't talk, no matter how hard I tried, but the commonly held belief was that this was a choice I was making. I didn't have the words to explain what was actually going on for me, and so when teachers, friends, even my parents asked me to shed some light on my silence, I had nothing to give them.

The simple truth was that in certain situations, my body became so anxious that I literally couldn't make a sound.

Most of the time I knew what I wanted to say, but something was preventing it from being spoken. It felt like a separation between body and mind – as though my body would not behave in its usual way, and certainly not the way I wanted it to. My tongue would sit in my mouth, and I literally had no idea how to make it form the words that I wanted to say. I knew that I *could* do this, and I knew where I needed to move my tongue inside of my mouth, but at the same time it felt heavy and clumsy and completely incapable of sounding out even one comprehensible word. My throat would grow tight, and no matter how hard I tried, words would not squeeze through.

For much of my life, it felt as though there was some kind of wall in my throat. Occasionally the gates would open, but most of the time it stood strong, holding many of my words away.

Over time, my words became tied up with emotions as well — and added to the anxiety that I clearly felt around speaking was a fear of what might come out when I actually did.

Anxiety is an interesting phenomenon. It manifests in different people in different ways, responding to the unique triggers we each have. I'm not sure if anyone was even aware that anxiety was fuelling my behavior as I opened and closed my mouth wordlessly, and gradually shrank further and further away from all of those conversations I was unable to have. For many years, I tried my hardest to push anxiety away. I did not want its presence in my life. I did not value its messages. I just felt like it was a nuisance, keeping me small and causing other people to judge me in ways that I did not like.

In an ideal world, anxiety is a healthy reaction to a life-threatening situation, but for some of us it can be triggered by the most seemingly insignificant things. To the logical mind anxiety doesn't make any sense, but to those of us who suffer, we battle with this nonsensical reality much of the time. We can feel shaky when the phone rings, let alone meeting people face to face and being expected to answer questions. Every day we step outside of our comfort zones over and over again; sometimes it is our choice, and we challenge ourselves to move forward – but other times it is the necessities of life in our society.

4. When you can't say what's wrong

The things we cannot say extend beyond pleasantries ...

S elective mutism comes with its obvious challenges. Being unable to speak in certain situations can be a cause for alarm, and is perceived to be something quite unusual. People react in a variety of ways toward the person who is mute – questions, judgment, acceptance ... However, as with any disability, until you actually suffer or know someone who does it is difficult to appreciate the many different ways it can affect life.

I have heard stories about children who become hurt at school but cannot tell anybody about it, and so their day is spent suffering in silence until they are able to go home and share their pain with their parents.

For myself, my most traumatic memory of being unable to speak up actually happened at home. Although for the most part, the anxiety surrounding speaking only happened outside of my home, if there were intense emotions involved, I found it impossible to speak no matter where I was.

I was three years old, sitting by our garage, playing by myself when I looked up and watched my younger brother (then eighteen months old) fall into our swimming pool. I knew he couldn't swim, and I had seen him fall into the deep end.

It didn't matter that I knew my parents would be close by; in that moment I was paralysed with fear and panic. Inside of me I was screaming for someone to help, but to the outside world I couldn't make a sound. I wanted to go and help him myself, but I found that not only could I not call for help, I also couldn't move.

I was devastated in that moment that I couldn't let my parents know that my brother was drowning. If anyone has ever been involved in a moment of intense fear and panic, they will know that sometimes things can seem to be moving in slow motion. Although it was only seconds before my dad dived in to save him, I had felt trapped in the fear and panic of not being able to do anything for my brother for what seemed to be much longer than this.

No one realized I had seen it all happen. While I watched my little brother as my parents helped him through his shock, I suffered silently, unable to tell anyone of what I had seen or the fears I had felt.

The inability to speak can bring about all kinds of unforeseen challenges in day-to-day life. One challenge that I faced daily as a child was going to the toilet. Asking my teacher caused me a huge amount of anxiety as it made me very uncomfortable that people knew what I was doing. Even when I could say other things, this was not something I could easily do.

Most of the time, I got around this problem by going to the toilet at play times and lunch time. I often structured my day by planning when I would go, so that I would never have to ask a teacher.

Unfortunately, things didn't always go to plan.

I was seven years old. I was really starting to need the toilet, and I was very much aware that it was a long time until our next break. Assembly was coming up, and if I didn't go before that I didn't know how long I could last.

I was summoning the courage to go and ask the teacher if I could go – only my teacher was really busy with some of the other kids, and I didn't dare go and say it in front of all those people. I looked into the class next door, and I decided I would go and ask that teacher instead.

I was sitting with my legs crossed tight, shifting around on my seat and daring myself to 'just do it!' In the next room, I noticed another child approach their teacher. I decided I would be next.

Just about to leave my seat, I hovered for a moment, when the teacher's voice sat me right back down again.

"Well, we all know you can go to the toilet, don't we – but that's not the question you should be asking me, is it? You should say, 'May I go to the toilet?' So, what was that again?"

I looked down and shifted myself again. I was stunned and realized that even if I could find a tiny whisper to say those words, my body wasn't about to walk me across the room to try it.

I felt stuck because just a few minutes later, we had to line up for assembly, and I was too scared to disappear now. I would just have to sit on my foot and hope that helped.

It didn't.

I feel like I left my body in that assembly ... in my memory, there is a dawning realization that someone is crying really loudly, and when I look around I can see that it is me. My heart sinks as I realize what I have done. I notice the puddle around my feet. One of the teachers ushers me out of the hall – in front of everybody. I feel deeply ashamed as I try to hide behind my hair and look down at my feet.

Not one part of me wanted to be there in that moment, and as I made my escape in my mind – shutting away the feelings and negative thoughts from my conscious awareness - a part of me remained forever trapped in the pain and shame of being unable to provide for myself the most basic of needs. I was intelligent and sensitive, and what I had just done made me feel worthless, useless, and much younger than my years.

This wasn't the first time, and it also wasn't the last. At eleven years old, I was again deeply ashamed and quite traumatized by the knowledge that I had had an opportunity to go, if I could only have found a way to ask. I was alone on this occasion, but walking home with the colour leaching out of my shoes onto my wet white socks as they squelched with every step was hugely humiliating. I don't know if anyone noticed, but I know that one teacher understood exactly what had happened. It didn't matter to me by then whether anyone else knew or not; I was beyond upset with myself, and my situation in life.

I had no idea why I couldn't talk sometimes. I longed to be able to spill everything out – all the pain, the frustration, the panic, and everything else. Every emotion, every word – I wanted to be free of it all as it swirled around inside of me, searching for its release.

Asking to go to the toilet was not the only question I had trouble asking. Over the years I have wondered many things inside of my head, but instead of sharing my curiosity with others, at the risk of exposing all the things I don't yet know, I preferred to work things out for myself.

I had to wait until I learned to drive before figuring out full-beam headlights (something that had puzzled me for a long time), and the ease with which the driver can switch them on and off. Every time we drove anyplace in the dark, I would wonder about this, trying to notice what my dad did to change the angle of our headlights. Inside of my head, I pleaded that my brother might one day ask my questions so I could satisfy my curiosity.

It wasn't only the full-beam question, I had many more too … some of them were even wordless inside of my mind. So much to know, so much to learn, and yet I found it virtually impossible and deeply traumatic to ask other people.

I was terrified that people might look down on me if I was to show them that I knew less than them. Sometimes, I heard people ask questions and they were laughed at for not already knowing the answer. The thought of this kind of response was unbearable to me.

In addition to asking questions that I didn't know the answers to, I also wasn't sure how to ask if I wanted something. I remember Nana asking me if I wanted some more dessert. She always asked me if I wanted more, and I was always grateful because I didn't have to ask. One visit my mum told Nana I could ask for it myself if I wanted it. I was torn. By now, I was easily in my mid-teens, and I wanted to believe that Mum was right. The thought that I could ask if I wanted something was an empowering one and something that I wanted to believe … but still, I was relieved when someone else did the asking for me.

5. School

School is the place where many children with selective mutism exhibit their strongest symptoms ...

As children we are expected to attend school - and for the selectively mute or anxious child, a day at school can be full of sensory overload and anxiety-provoking experiences. Every day we go to school, we enter a situation that is far outside of our comfort zone. It's bad enough walking into the classroom, but once we are there we are expected to answer the roll, engage with our teachers and peers, ask to go to the toilet, and much more. I imagine every school is a little different in their understanding and approach toward selective mutism. My feeling is that, because school is such a large part of our lives as children, then the way selective mutism is tackled could make all the difference.

At my school in the 1980s, there was no recommended approach and no support offered to my parents. I was just another child in a fairly large class, and there was only one girl in my class whom I could talk to. If I needed to say something, I would whisper it to her. School wasn't a terrible experience for me, but it definitely had its moments! When I think back to my time at school, I shrink a little. I feel small, and I know that I played small when I was there.

I usually went home for lunch as we lived just a few houses down the road from my primary school – and this gave me a break from the challenges of school in the middle of the day. Occasionally, however, I had to stay at school, and on this particular day my class were on 'Last Dinners'.

I looked at the menu for the day and spent my time lining up desperately hoping that something nice would be left by the time I got to choose. When I reached the window I was not really surprised to find that all the good food had already been taken. I had already worked out how I would react in every possible scenario while I was waiting because I didn't like drawing attention to myself when I was trying to make a decision. I surveyed the empty platters and quickly pointed to the only thing I felt I would be able to stomach. Usually I liked mashed potato, but the school mash was lumpy and came from a packet. Still, it was the best choice up there, so that was what I was having.

"Would you like anything else?" the Dinner Lady asked me. I looked at the pile of soggy cabbage and shook my head and was about to leave when a teacher spotted my bare plate.

I was terrified of this particular teacher, especially at lunch times. She would often walk around telling children off for holding their knives and forks in the wrong hands. I always checked how the kids on my table were holding their knives and forks so she couldn't catch me out. Unfortunately, on this particular day, she spotted my tray and its measly portion of mashed potato.

Immediately she was on my case and started to insist that I must eat something else as well. Of course, I couldn't tell her that I didn't like anything else and that this would be fine for me today, so after a few shaken heads from me and some frustrated questioning from her, she instructed the Dinner Lady to add another lump of mash to my plate. As I was about to walk away, she insisted that I should eat something for dessert as well. My stomach lurched as I realized that there was only custard left for dessert. If I didn't really like the school's mashed potato, I especially didn't like their custard.

While I ate, the teacher watched me like a hawk, and she sat me back down three times to eat more. I felt sick and could barely swallow – and by the time I got started on my custard, I was literally gagging. I don't remember if I actually threw up right there in the dining room, but I wouldn't be surprised if I did.

I think, in this situation, selective mutism made everything worse than it needed to be. I wasn't the only child who was scared of this particular teacher, but I was the only child who couldn't say a word to her. Sometimes I wonder how it would have been if the teachers at my school had known what selective mutism was. How different might my experience of school have been if there had been a therapeutic approach?

I remember one day watching a girl who had cerebral palsy as she walked through our classroom with her teacher aide. I remember thinking that I longed to have a more obvious disability ... I found it very challenging to have such an acute understanding of everything that was going on, but being unable to express my reaction to it. I longed to have someone who was there to help me in school – someone who understood me, and could help me to navigate my days with a little less overwhelm.

Today, many children with selective mutism are assigned a teacher aide for part of their week. The sliding-in technique is also often adopted. This technique introduces speaking in small, manageable steps at a pace which is set by the child. It usually begins by taking the child into a situation in which they feel comfortable. Gradually, other people or settings are introduced, so that the child's anxieties have the space to adjust and decrease. It is also important that alongside sliding in, other teachers and adults who come into contact with the child are educated about what selective mutism is and the best way to support the child's confidence.

I imagine how different things might have been for me if this technique and the developed understandings we now have had been common practice and knowledge in the early '80s. How different might it be for the many, many children who still face the lack of understanding that I did thirty years ago? How much easier would it be for the parents who feel they have to fight and advocate for their children? How much more satisfying might it be for teachers to see these children relax and shine?

Sliding in provides the acknowledgement and acceptance that I used to crave ... working at a pace inside which the child feels comfortable means that the child feels heard and in control of their progress. I appreciate that sliding in would take considerable resources and time, but it could also completely transform the experience of school and anxiety for the child with selective mutism.

School is a place where children spend a lot of time – it makes sense to me that working toward reducing anxiety at school will provide the best chance of overcoming all selective mutism symptoms.

Despite my difficulties, school was a place where I excelled in many ways. I was intelligent, and I was recognised for my creative abilities. My first teacher once pointed out that I was the only five-year-old she had taught who could draw in perspective. If I had my way I would have spent every day drawing and making things – with a bit of writing time too. Unfortunately, this isn't the way school is set up, and despite the fact that every report I received was good, I only noticed the bit where my teacher pointed out how quiet I was. I wished I could have been happy with the good bits, but my association with 'quiet' meant that it overshadowed everything else for me.

If I could share one thing that I wish had been done differently through my childhood it would be the framing of 'quiet'. I always heard it as a problem, and I didn't know any differently. Because quiet was a problem, I thought that I was a problem. I thought that I needed to change who I was so that other people would accept me.

6. Why are you so quiet?

If you find yourself asking this question, don't expect an answer!

There is nothing that has had as large an impact upon my life as the word, 'quiet'. I grew up avoiding and disliking it - flinching each time I heard it and longing to hear a different adjective being used in my direction. At the same time I embodied 'quiet' and simply could not get away from it no matter how hard I tried.

I had developed a belief that 'quiet' meant problems. 'Quiet' meant wrong. 'Quiet' meant there was something I needed to change or improve. As long as I was quiet I felt that I could never be good enough, but fighting against it was the same as fighting against myself.

One day, just a few years ago, I was preparing to take my children home after a day of school skiing. The area was busy, and people were bustling to and fro. I stood to the side with my son -

waiting for my daughter to finish up in the rentals department, and idly watched the crowds of people as they flooded past me.

The conversations were varied and flowed into each other. They made very little sense, and I was enjoying my lazy observations. Suddenly, out of nowhere I was plucked out of my comfortable, dreamy space and shocked into a whirlwind of pain as five words cut through my heart like a knife,

"Why are you so quiet?"

My eyes grew wide and I stared at the woman who had said it, feeling shocked and stunned and not at all like the thirty-four-year-old mum I had grown accustomed to being.

She was waiting for her answer. I was confused and scared, and I noticed the gamut of emotions that had risen inside of me. I struggled to maintain any kind of balance as I was whisked back and forth between this moment here and many others in the past. Blinking away the confusion, I took a breath and refocused. I looked back at the woman, and then I noticed that she was looking at a young boy of about ten. Her face was fixed and requested an answer as they walked side by side. Her words were demanding, cutting, hurting.

The boy's eyes were aimed low. His head hung from rounded shoulders, and he shuffled along like he didn't really want to be there.

My heart reached out to him. I wanted to hug him; I wanted to help him. I wanted to be his voice and to tell the woman how difficult her question can be to answer.

I wanted her to know how much her opinion hurts; I wanted to make her aware of the struggles people like me and probably that young boy faced.

I had my chance to say it. Right in front of me was an opportunity to show myself how far I had come since my childhood. That moment felt like forever. The rush of people flooding past had slowed to an almost stop.

But so had I.

The woman and the boy were strangers to me, but in that moment their situation impacted on me hugely. I found myself taken away. One moment I had been a mum, capable and confident. The next moment I was a child, wide-eyed and vulnerable, staring at my teacher's feet with my heart pounding and not a single word able to pass the impossible wall inside of my throat.

"I should be able to say something!" the grown-up part of me thought. I longed to prove - to myself and the world - how far I had come.

I learned that I hadn't really come anywhere.

I was still the small child I once had been, entirely unable to utter a sound.

Slowly, the memories faded, and I found myself back in the moment. The opportunity was gone – hurried away by the crowd. I took a deep breath, blinked back my tears, and with heart still pounding I took my son's hand. Together we set off to find my daughter.

It was a huge shock for me to learn that I hadn't

really changed in many ways. Although I could appear to be confident, mature, and fully grown, when it really came down to it, there was very little difference between my grown-up and childhood feelings. In this case they seemed to be one and the same. I had travelled straight back to a time in my childhood where that question had had the exact same impact ...

> I was thirteen years old. My maths teacher asked me to stay behind after class. I was a little shocked but did as I was told, and when the other kids had left, she turned to me.
>
> **"Why are you so quiet, Kathryn?"**
>
> She asked me gently, and I could see from the way she stood that she felt concerned and longed to be able to help, but concern wasn't what I needed. I was desperate for people to accept the way I was and to acknowledge how much I did do.
> It was such an effort for me to go to school every day, to sit in my classes, to answer the roll, to navigate my friendships, to go to the toilet, to answer questions, to speak in a voice that wasn't questioned or laughed at, and then to try my very best to fit in ... Instead of noticing how much effort it was for me to do what I already was doing and acknowledging that, people instead turned to me with their soft expressions and gentle voices, and all I heard were accusations. I heard people questioning my nature, the very way I was, and their questions ripped through my heart.
> "What is wrong with me? Why am I like this?

Why can't I answer a simple question?"

But to me, the question wasn't simple, and I couldn't answer it.

My teacher had a deep desire to help me and to understand. I could see it in her eyes – searching, hopeful, desperate to make a difference. I wished I could give her what she wanted. I longed to speak my answer. I longed to know my answer.

I grew up hearing 'quiet' mentioned alongside feelings of concern, and I came to the conclusion that it must be a problem. The concern and the questions echoed inside of my body, and my understanding of 'quiet' became hugely confused and distorted.

Inside of my mind is a rich and busy world, filled with unspoken words, wishes, and imaginings. Living inside of a mind that has often found it very difficult to express and make sense of itself, I felt anything but quiet.

People's questions took on the added dimension of confusion in my young mind. Quiet seemed to be cause for concern, an indication that something must be wrong. People described me as 'quiet' all the time, but at the same time my mind was noisy and full. My sense of self became trapped somewhere between these two contradictions.

This confusion consumed me for three decades, as I sought ways to hide my natural personality and instead present myself as a capable, confident, friendly person who can easily fit into any situation.

In this way, I found out that denying your true nature and constantly striving to be someone you are not is an exhausting, unfulfilling way to go about your days.

It is only this year that my opinion of 'quiet' has truly changed. Up until I started blogging about selective mutism, I was feeling proud that 'quiet' was not a word I heard mentioned very much anymore. Unfortunately, anytime that I did hear it, I would frame it in a negative context, and my body would physically recoil from it.

I wrote about it on my blog and explored what 'quiet' actually is if you peel back the outer shell and discover what it holds inside. I discovered a colourful tapestry of imagination, awareness, empathy, and depth. I realized that by pushing away 'quiet', I was limiting my potential to share my best qualities.

Without 'quiet' I couldn't be the sensitive, considerate, observant, capable, creative, imaginative, and passionate person that I am.

This is a realization that has literally changed my life and the way I think about myself. I will expand upon it in part two of this book.

7. Smile!

Non-verbal communication can be tricky too

When I tune in, I often notice a slight tension in my body. It is very subtle, but it is usually there, holding me back and inhibiting my expressions.

> *During my first driving lesson, after figuring out the gears, the clutch, and the brakes, I went for my first ever drive around some roads. It felt fantastic – to be in control of this car for the first time, and my driving instructor was obviously tuned into the first-time driver's feelings.*
>
> *"Are you enjoying yourself?"*
> *"Yes!"*
> *"Well, smile then!"*
>
> *Inside of myself I was beaming, but the intensity of my feeling was somehow lost in translation so that I sat a little stiffly and wore an*

expression of sensible concentration.

The smile I gave him was forced. Although I wore a very large, genuine smile inside of my body, I literally couldn't place it on my face.

It feels as though there is often a layer of protection around me — something that prevents me from transparently sharing all that I am. It is here most of the time, but is especially activated in any kind of emotionally overwhelming situation. I often feel a little stiff and uncomfortable in my expressions and movements, regardless of what I am actually feeling inside. I find it extremely difficult to give everything away, but ironically, this is also something that I long to do.

I adore the bubbling emotions of my children and others who share their feelings uncontrollably. It makes me light up inside — to see a person's thoughts and feelings written all over their face and body and to witness the freedom with which they are able to share themselves. At the same time, it scares me to think that other people might also read me so easily.

When parents talk about their children, they often share with delight, or laughter, this kind of bubbling expression. Somewhere inside, I don't like to be talked about like this (even though observing it in others makes me smile so much.) I don't like to draw extra attention to who I am, and so my unconscious set point appears to be to hide my truth. Instead of shining with all that I am, I dull down my expressions.

Over the years, I have gotten very good at expressing myself in a way that isn't fully me but is able to satisfy others. It does not always come from me — but it is enough to show, for example, the driving instructor that I am actually enjoying myself.

When I went to university, a friend called me the "Girl of a thousand faces." He didn't realize that what he was seeing was my attempt to mask over my true feelings. He had no idea of how much I was holding back and how many of my expressions had been learned and forced in their own way.

I seem to have an in-built barometer that requires me to tone down my excitement or mask over my fears, and I'm not really sure why.

As I grow, I am learning to share more and more of myself, and it is my goal to become completely free with this. I don't want to hold anything back – I want to be transparent and readable, the way that other people are for me.

Returning to my younger days, before I learned to fake a smile, a noticeable characteristic of my selective mutism was my difficulty in smiling for the camera. If one of my parents were behind the lens, it was usually okay, although only if no one else was watching. Being photographed by anyone else I found that it was literally impossible for me to smile.

I am reminded of a photograph of my brother and me when we were perhaps five and three. My younger brother followed my lead, and so we are both sitting there looking as solemn as can be. I don't know how many attempts the photographer took in an attempt to find a smile, but we have sat on the sideboard at my parents' house like this for years.

A smile to the camera is incredibly difficult when your body is preventing you from doing it. Given a choice, it would have been so much easier to plant a fake smile in the direction of the camera than facing all of that coaxing and disappointment from the photographer, but I had to relax a certain amount before faking a smile was even possible.

Anxiety had me looking stiff, solemn, and unhappy, regardless of what was actually going on inside of me. Behind that expression could just as easily have been anger as joy, but anxiety prevented any of that from revealing itself.

The difficulty for me was always magnified when I was encouraged to smile. Being told that what I was doing was 'not good enough' added pressure and anxiety to the already overloaded situation. I know it must be difficult to only gain photographs of your visually solemn, sad-looking child, but if you want to improve the situation, my advice would be to enjoy what you do have. Asking an anxious, frozen child to smile will not achieve your desired result, and coaxing is most likely to push them further away. One suggestion I have would be to ask your child if they mind if you take photographs when they are playing, without their awareness of the camera. If they say yes, then you can get some wonderful, natural shots with zero tension or effort. Be wary of not asking, though, because I would have felt a little betrayed in this situation.

A similar difficulty that I experienced as a child and

sometimes notice today is eye contact.

The communication that can go on when two people's eyes meet blows me away. I long for the connection that eye contact provides, but at the same time it can be difficult for me to maintain eye contact with people for very long. It feels like I am staring right inside of a person – right into their soul. It brings about a huge emotional response inside of me, and I can quickly slip into overwhelm, especially when I am not prepared.

By the same token, when a person looks at my eyes, even when I do not look back, it can feel like they are drilling a hole right inside of me. The light that shines from a person's eyes can be like the sun – sometimes I feel like I need to protect my eyes, especially if I feel ashamed or not yet ready to share whatever it is they are trying to ask me about or understand. I know that one glance in their direction could reveal everything, and I am not necessarily ready to feel that exposed.

Eye contact is a monumental thing – and the more sensitive a person is, the more communication I imagine we can sense through the eyes.

8. Food and other sensitivities

There's a lot of expectation in 'Just try it!'

I have always avoided eating dairy products, much to my mum's frustration! I'm not sure why, but something about milk and cheese just doesn't feel good to me. As an adult I sometimes eat a little bit of dairy, and I almost always feel bloated afterward. It has never been official, but I suspect that I avoided dairy as a child because of a mild intolerance. Plus I never enjoyed the taste.

I am reminded of my mum's attempts to get me to try new things.

"But tastes change! Maybe you might like it now!"

One glance at a plate of mushrooms and I could tell that I wasn't going to like them. I could almost feel their weird texture inside of my mouth just by looking at them.

Texture, smell, taste … eating is a sensory experience, and for people (like me) who are sensitive to new experiences, I recommend treading carefully.

But it wasn't only the taste, the texture, and the

smell ... for me and possibly other selective mute children, a major factor in trying new things was the attention it attracted.

Even worse for me as a child than trying something new was trying something new while people watched me. There was always an undercurrent of anticipation around the table; it felt as though everyone was waiting for my reaction as they wavered between their expectation that I would refuse and the hope that I might eat and enjoy it.

I felt like I was under a lot of pressure, and because of this, regardless of what the new thing was, I couldn't really taste it. My mouth felt funny, my tongue felt big, and my throat felt closed. It was difficult to swallow, and my anxiety was high. Attention and expectation pushed my anxiety levels up in a place where I usually felt comfortable and at ease.

> *I could feel eyes on me. I could feel the unspoken questions – wondering if I might eat it this time. I didn't want to please, and I didn't want to disappoint. I just wanted to be left alone to try new things when I was ready ... and by myself!*

If you have a fussy eater, I hope you will consider the possibility that focusing on their reaction to new food might be making it more difficult for your child to try new things.

One recommendation I have here is to introduce new things when your child is able to explore it on their own. If you make them platters of food for morning or afternoon tea, maybe you could add something new? You do not need to draw any kind of attention to the new food, and definitely try to steer clear of expectation. Simply put it down and walk away. Do not become too attached about whether the new food is eaten or not – or even whether it has been picked up. If your child does not mention it, maybe you could bring it up at a time when they are feeling relaxed ...

"Did you notice the (new thing) I put on your plate today?"

... And then leave it to your child to continue the conversation – or not.

As a child I was a fussy eater, and today as a mum, I have a fussy eater for a child. I am therefore aware of the frustrations it can bring to both sides of the table.

I have found that letting go of my natural tendency to try to control my son's eating habits has worked wonders. I always offer him a balanced range of foods, but I have eased the pressure for him to eat or try new things by steering clear of expectations and hope. I respect his desires, and from time to time I find myself pleasantly surprised when his plate returns to me empty with his smiling face asking for more! It is in these moments that I realize that my son knows his own body, and if there is something that he particularly needs, he will eat it if it is available to him.

On another tangent, I definitely notice a connection between the food I eat and my anxiety levels. This also includes the way I eat my food, and the way I feel about the food I eat. I have realized that it matters if I am giving myself time to sit down and enjoy my food, or if I am in a hurry and grab something easy as I run out of the door. It is also important that I feel okay about whatever I am eating. This means that if I think I shouldn't be eating something, I usually feel worse afterward than if I eat the same food but choose to savour and enjoy it.

I began a course on nutrition about seven years ago, but after reading some very interesting books and learning some fascinating information I felt that I knew even less than I did before! I was overwhelmed by how much there is to know and understand about our bodies, and I chose instead to trust my intuition about food for myself and my children – and to not become a nutritionist!

Nutrition is a massive subject, and one that I do not feel comfortable to delve into here. However, I do think it's something that I would encourage you to explore by yourself if you aren't already, and see what resonates. Our bodies are all made so differently, and what works for one person may not have the same affect in another – I guess that's why there are so many different and conflicting recommendations available to us today. If you are looking for a starting point, I would recommend that you cut down on processed foods and introduce more whole, organic, home-made alternatives – and try your best to ignore the hype.

9. Aiming for normality

The sacrifice of who you are versus the desire to fit in …

After I had been at school for a little while, I began to develop a dream. It was not a lofty goal, but for me it meant the world.

I wanted to feel the way that I imagined other people felt about themselves. I wanted to be able to express myself effortlessly like them - to speak my mind, to share my thoughts, to move through my life with the apparent ease of everybody else.

'Normal' is a goal that so many of us strive to achieve when we are young. The dream of fitting in, of finding acceptance from others … when I was seven years old I could not imagine anything better! When we grow, we learn that we can only achieve these things by walking away from 'normal' and embracing the person we already are, but when our self-esteem is suffering then normal seems like the ultimate achievement. Unfortunately, it is also the most elusive goal I can imagine — because it means something different to each of us, and its boundaries keep moving.

I used to long to look at my teachers and not to notice the concern that flickered behind their delight at my latest beautiful drawing. I wished they could enjoy my picture for all that it was, without the afterthought that *'If only she could talk as well as she can draw'*.

I knew that my parents were concerned too, and I wished I could be normal so they didn't have to worry about me.

There were times when my parents asked me to try to tell them what was happening for me. They wanted to understand why I could talk sometimes and couldn't at other times. They wanted to help me – but I didn't know how to ask them for the help I wanted.

All I wanted was for someone to accept me completely the way I was. I wanted someone who never felt any need to question me – who would completely allow me to be whoever I needed to be in each moment.

I wanted them to <u>not</u> feel they had to ask me. I wanted them to <u>not</u> feel there was anything about me that needed to change. I wanted them to feel completely okay with the way I was – so that they could show me how to do that for myself.

It's a big ask.

I wanted my parents to understand my needs. I wanted them to know that I wasn't choosing to not speak … but it was just too difficult for me to tell them.

There was too much emotion in the way.

I couldn't tell them what I wanted to say so desperately.

I am who I need to be right now.

I always felt I had to explain myself, to make excuses for my differences so that I might make sense to other people. I didn't realize back then that their misunderstandings were their problems. I took them on as my own and added to my load of difference.

In my opinion there was only one way out. I needed to be more normal.

When I look back, I wish I could have celebrated myself for the person I was and the talents I was able to share. I was incredible at drawing, writing, and pretty much anything creative. I was intelligent, and I could beat most of the boys in my class at chess. I was caring and often sold pictures I had drawn or things I had made so I could give money to charity. I was particularly drawn to helping endangered animals. I was incredibly flexible and physically capable. I was good at running, swimming, and gymnastics.

I had a lot to offer, a lot to give, and a lot to share.

Despite all of this, I couldn't escape the one thing that was missing. I wasn't normal. I couldn't talk like other people, and even if I could, I was terrified of who might overhear me.

It freaked me out that other people might hear my voice when we were singing. In every assembly ever I have either stayed out of my teacher's line of sight or mouthed the words to songs. We weren't allowed to not sing. Occasionally I would attempt to let a little sound escape – daring myself to sing like everybody else.

"l-a"

It was barely audible, and yet to me it sounded so loud. That 'l-a' echoed inside me as it vibrated through my body. I regretted it instantly, and kept on mouthing the rest of the song as I looked around at everyone else.

I was terrified. Someone must have heard me – it sounded so loud! I waited for the judgment to come, the sideways glances, the frowns, the steps to the side.

I couldn't believe that no one seemed to notice that I had just made a sound. I could hear everyone else, and as I listened I noticed that they all seemed to be okay with it. The tuneful, the loud booming voices, the gentle voices, the out-of-tune and the shrill notes. I heard it all, and I was in awe that all these other people had no problem with singing out loud and letting everyone else hear their voice.

I didn't like people to hear my voice, even when everyone else was talking or singing above it. It terrified me to imagine what people might think of me.

Singing was easy to sort out though – I stayed small, hid behind my hair and when I was able to I mouthed the words, and it looked like I was singing. No one seemed to notice, or care, that I wasn't really doing it.

Speaking was something that I desperately wanted

to do – no matter what the cost. At seven years old I was becoming more and more aware of the way other people viewed me. No longer did my friends believe the 'Africa' story. Sometimes I felt people thought I was special because I couldn't talk, and somehow I seemed to be attracting even more attention to me because of this. One thing that I really didn't like was having the attention on me, especially regarding a trait that I couldn't control. I knew that if I could talk just a little, this spotlight would move; its brightness and pressure would be relieved.

In many ways, I longed to wait for my voice to emerge when it was ready. I knew that I would not always find it so difficult to speak.

However, I had absolutely no idea how long this process might take – and I didn't feel I could cope with the added pressure that might mount in that time.

The key came when I realized that if I could pretend to sing, maybe I could pretend to speak too. Speaking to elicit the least possible reaction and to meet the expectations of others demands a lot less pressure than speaking because I am ready to. I had a pretty good idea what people were hoping to hear – and so, bit by bit, that is what they got. I experimented with speaking a little so that I could ease the pressure I was feeling. I pushed words out, and although it took tremendous effort, I found that it did serve to shrink the focus I felt in my direction.

Although I wasn't yet ready to use my own words, I could meet my basic needs by saying only the bare minimum of what was expected from me. I felt like I was pretending that I could speak, because it didn't feel like me who was talking, but somehow I managed to say enough to relieve the pressure and spotlight I had been hoping to shrink away from.

Over time, I gradually formed a habit of meeting people's expectations and speaking just enough so that I might fit in. It was a hugely unsatisfying way to communicate – I had started this because I wanted to experience acceptance and I wanted to fit in, but the more years that went by, the less I felt like I accomplished my goals. My voice was not my own – it seemd to come from a place that was forced – it was quite shallow and felt like the top of my throat. Most of the time I spoke words to gain the approval of others, not because I felt compelled to speak them.

The goal of normal was like the proverbial carrot – dangling right in front of my nose but never close enough for me to actually bite.

10. What if someone hears me?

The fear of being overheard by a stranger can be paralysing ...

Once I started speaking a little bit outside of my home, it was established that I could do it. I was unable, back then, to explain to anybody how difficult it was – and I certainly couldn't express the fact that when I was at school I was only pretending to talk.

It was therefore very difficult for my parents to understand when we went out and my voice disappeared. I remember talking as loudly as I physically could. I would make a huge effort, and the result would be a tiny whisper, my words fluttering out and dissolving into the air. I literally felt like I was shouting, and it was hugely deflating to go to all that effort only to be asked to repeat it because my parents couldn't hear what I was saying.

> *When I was about eight, I remember having saved up some of my pocket money. There was a shop close to our house that I loved to browse, and so many things that I wanted in there. On this*

particular day, I went to spend my pocket money there with my parents.

The shop was small, and I was all too aware of the shop assistant at the desk. There were also other people in the shop. I was terrified that I might be overheard by someone if I spoke to my parents, but they kept asking me what I wanted to buy.

My answer came in a barely audible whisper. It was an extreme effort for me to get this out, and I was feeling overwhelmed by the sheer effort that it had taken to choke out those small sounds.

My parents had hardly heard me. They gently urged me to speak a little louder. It felt like the tears were running through the insides of my body. The pressure and pain were insurmountable – and it seemed absolutely impossible to try again. This is where the memory fades. I'm not sure what I bought that day – or even if I did manage to say something else. I do, however, have many other happy memories of leaving that shop with something special in my hands.

It is a very difficult thing to explain ... the idea of a person hearing my voice, the fear of their judgment, the overwhelming anxiety that threatens to crush my sense of self as I use every ounce of my energy to attempt to say something audible. The pressure feels immense – I am desperate to say something, if only to ease the pressure, but when I do I fear that words and emotions will come bursting out like a shaken-up bottle of pop.

When anxiety has held your words back for a long time, it is not quite so simple as suddenly talking. Inside there becomes a buildup of sorts ... words and feelings all tangled up and all wanting to express themselves. Those words and feelings don't care how they sound; they just want to be heard. I think it's because of this that I have developed the habit of changing the way I behave depending on who might be listening.

Since becoming a parent, I noticed that the way I talked to my children would change depending on who was within earshot. I felt completely happy to be myself, no matter how I was feeling, when only my children were around, but add somebody else to the mix and suddenly my behavior would change radically. Along with my behavior, my voice would change too. The habit of wanting to appear to be confident meant that my pretend voice would come out around other people, and I noticed that when I talked to my children in public settings, my focus was scattered between them and other people close by.

I was quite shocked when I first noticed this, and wondered what they made of my differing behavior.

As a parent, I believe it is hugely important that you model the behavior you would like to see.

I wanted to encourage my children to be themselves in every situation, but my behavior was teaching them how to adjust yourself and your behavior depending on where you are and who is there. My children teach me so much about myself, it simply blows me away. They also help me to expand outside of my old comfortable place. In this situation, my desire to act as a stronger role model for my children was the catalyst I needed to be myself in more and more settings. The fear of being overheard has been overshadowed by the fear of my children taking on my 'negative' characteristics.

It is my opinion that the balance of this weight of fears and desires is an important factor in changing behavior.

Transformation can only occur when the desire to change becomes a greater force than the fear that holds you back.

This means that if you aren't getting what you want, or being who you want to be, you simply need to want it more, so that it tips the balance of whatever is stopping you. A person who wants something above anything else will do almost anything to achieve it. I didn't understand this for a long time, because I thought that I wanted to change more than anything else. I didn't think it was possible to want anything more. I hoped and I dreamed and I wished … but at the same time I didn't allow myself to feel or acknowledge my fears and anxieties about what might happen if I were to change.

The magic bullet, for me, was when I started to feel my fears as much as I felt my wants. I realized that my subconscious mind had been holding on tightly to the fear I had of changing into the person I so desperately wanted to be. Until I recognized this, no amount of wanting was ever enough. I realized that you have to want what you want enough that you will allow yourself to really see why you don't have it. When you truly realize that it is only you who stands in your way of getting your desire, no matter how things might appear, you take back your power and that's when the magic happens.

11. Complications of Selective Mutism

Eating disorders, depression, alcohol ...

Navigating my teens was no easy feat ... I had spent a few years pretending that I could talk at school, and my sense of self was pretty low. If fitting in had been important before, suddenly it was paramount. I was envious of some people in my school who seemed perfectly capable of being their imperfect selves, and I longed to be able to do the same ... but the idea of showing myself as someone who literally couldn't talk felt scarier than saying the few pretend things I was able to.

It is understood today that without early intervention and the opportunity to develop skills to manage anxiety, selective mutism can become an ingrained behaviour or lead to further difficulties. In my teens and early adult years, my experience certainly followed this pattern. I feel it is important to note here that everybody's experience in life is different. Just because I faced the difficulties I'm about to share does not mean that this is a likely outcome for you or your child if appropriate early action is not taken. This is simply my story – and this is the part where my long-held insecurities and unresolved anxieties mixed with the changes and developments that happened in my teenage years.

Through my childhood, I gradually started to feel more and more trapped inside of my behavior. No matter how hard I tried, I couldn't be the person I wanted to be.

> # I felt like my life was not my own – more the product of my situation - which felt like it was beyond my control.

School was becoming more difficult. I was bullied by some of my friends and teased when I moved in different circles. I was still questioned about my quietness, a trait that I felt I should have long before outgrown. I didn't feel like I had control over anything – my difficult emotions were almost impossible to express, even at home - and so eventually, at the age of sixteen, facing the additional pressure of exams, I began to control the only thing I felt like I could.

Food.

> *I prepared my own breakfast, chose my own lunch, and ate dinner with my family. Reducing the amount of food I was eating was a method I used to feel like I had some kind of control over my life. I*

began to notice my body responding to this, and it felt good because I knew exactly how it had happened. I was eating less, and my body was becoming skinnier. It wasn't that I had any concerns about my weight or the way my body looked ... it was simply that I enjoyed experiencing this element of control over an aspect of my life.

I wrote a lot at this stage of my life – to help me to arrange my thoughts and make sense of all that I was feeling. I remember comparing myself to people with anorexia and feeling like this was something very different because my motivation wasn't to lose weight. I simply enjoyed seeing my body's response to a choice that I was able to make. I liked it, and it became addictive.

After about two months, Mum noticed that I wasn't eating much, and she probably also noticed my size. She talked to me about it – and suddenly the joy I had been feeling around my new-found control dissolved. I felt silly and naïve. I couldn't explain it to Mum, and I began to feel guilty that I had wanted to experience this feeling of control. Further feelings of having been misunderstood surfaced, as I realized that she had no idea about my motivations behind eating less. I knew I was skinny – and I liked my body. I hadn't ever wanted to lose any weight, but now that I didn't have food to control, I once again felt helpless.

When I think back to this difficult time in my life, I wish I could say that this helped me to wake up, seize control of my life in a healthy way, and gain back my sense of self … but it didn't. In truth, this was only the beginning as I learnt how to navigate my shaky ship into adulthood.

> *One night, toward the end of my GCSE exams, I got drunk for the first time. I had never before felt so free of inhibition. That night I had a lot of fun. I talked to people I had never spoken to before. I danced, I laughed, and I probably sang too.*
>
> *Later that week, I overheard a girl I really respected talking about me.*
>
> *"If you're having a party, you have to invite Kathryn! She's so funny when she's drunk!!"*
>
> *I had never heard anyone talk about me in this way. I had never considered myself to be funny either – but in that moment, something changed for me. I felt like I had just taken a giant leap toward the elusive 'normal' that I had begun chasing so long ago. I didn't give it away, but inside I wore a huge smile. I felt like I was finally gaining acceptance, and it felt amazing!*

In this way, alcohol became a part of my life. It seemed to give me a freedom that I had only before been able to imagine, and even in my sober state I started to gain confidence. The next year I had made a lot of changes in my life. I started sixth form college in the next town and was attempting to start again, in a sense. I made new friends, had a part-time job, and was developing quite an active social life. I felt like I was beginning to take control as I made choices for myself that felt exciting.

I thought things were looking up for me. In many ways I was leading a very different life than I ever had before, and it seemed to have happened so quickly. What I didn't pay attention to was the fact that I was also pushing away a lot of burgeoning emotions.

Despite my growing confidence, I was also feeling really fragile. Perhaps I was trying to do too much too soon; maybe life was moving too quickly for my sensitive temperament – or maybe I was going in the wrong direction?

I started to feel as though I was watching my life through a fogged-up window. I looked like me, but I wasn't feeling very connected to some of the things I did or said. When I went out drinking, I often forgot large chunks of the evening. Pieces of my life started to crumble, and I wondered, once again, what was wrong with me. How was it that I was gaining the acceptance and normality that I had craved for so long, and yet nothing about it felt good?

As a seventeen-year-old, I went to the doctor and told him how I was feeling. Five minutes later I walked out with a prescription for something not dissimilar to Prozac.

Looking back, I am shocked and upset that a doctor could be so quick to hand out drugs. What I was told was,

"Keep doing what you are doing. Take these pills and you'll feel better!"

And so I did. Three months later I did feel better,

and under the doctor's advice I started to wean myself off the medication.

I do believe that medication has its place, and for some people it can literally make life worth living ... but for me, I think I could have used a therapist before I went down this route. It took me six months before I was medication-free – because every three days I could hardly stand up I felt so dizzy! In the end, I had to just throw the pills away and endure two weeks of dizziness, nausea, and mood swings.

Following this, I have dipped in and out of depression a few times, but I've never returned to a doctor's office about it. For about eight years, I self-medicated with alcohol. I liked the confidence that alcohol gave me, and it also helped me to push away my doubts and fears. However, as I grew older, I started to experience some nasty hangovers. I would awaken feeling sick, dizzy, and overwhelmed by feelings of guilt and shame. I had no idea what I had done that made me feel so bad – and on catching up with friends, I would find out that there literally wasn't anything to feel guilty for. But the feeling lingered. Only alcohol could take it away.

I think I hid my addiction to alcohol quite effectively – but I did have some friends asking me why I drank so much, and why I found it so difficult to stop. The truth was, I didn't even know myself. I just felt compelled to stay out late and drink myself away from my world. Looking back now, it is clear to me that I was avoiding something, and the feelings that consumed me when I woke up were a clue, but I had no idea back then of how far I was side-stepping the life I really wanted to be living.

From the age of twenty-four, my dependence on alcohol started to decline, mainly due to my relationship with Simon and the new sense of security that I was beginning to feel. I drank my last sip at the age of twenty-seven, shortly before I became pregnant for the first time. Sometimes people are shocked to hear that I don't drink at all. I don't fill them in on the details, but to me this is a decision I made for my mental, emotional, physical, and spiritual health and I am proud of myself for choosing it. It is clear to me that alcohol pulled me away from the person I had always longed to be, and if I was still drinking today, I'm fairly sure my life would look massively different than the way it looks right now!

12. How far do I have to run?

The irony of running from myself, only to find that there is nowhere else to go ...

Returning to the age of sixteen, I would like to tell a different aspect of my life as I became an adult. At this age I realized that for the first time in my life, I felt ready to take control of my life and my destiny.

I had had enough of being quiet. I felt that I could never change as long as the people around me knew who I was and where I was coming from. I don't remember it being a difficult decision to choose a sixth form college in a different town – a place where nobody knew who I was. I was focused and I was excited. I was making a big decision for myself, and through it I felt hugely empowered.

By making this decision I saw an opportunity to reinvent myself.

I thought it would be easy – I had been watching other people for years, and I knew the traits I wanted to associate myself with. I wanted to be confident and fun. I wanted to speak easily and often. I wanted to be friendly and easygoing. Most of all, I wanted to know how it felt to not be quiet.

> *I remember that first day at college - lining up with the other students as we figured out our classes and where we needed to go. Everyone else seemed to know each other. I felt incredibly alone, but I put on a brave face and tried to appear confident. I longed to be able to talk to someone – anyone – but initiating conversation was still incredibly difficult for me.*
>
> *So I stood there, waiting to hear where I had to go, watching everybody else as they laughed and joked together.*

A friend has since told me that she wanted to approach me that day, but she thought by the way I was standing that I seemed to think I was better than everybody else. At the time she noticed my fake confident body language and mistook it for arrogance. I was trying so hard that day to be someone who I wasn't. I was desperately trying to prove myself, but instead I was overlaying my insecurities with qualities that I wasn't yet ready to embody.

In my time at that college I made some great friends. I had my first boyfriend. My heart was broken for the first time, and I suffered my first bout of depression. I socialized a lot, and I found people who enjoyed being around me. But, at the end of the day, people still called me quiet.

I was far from my goal, and so at nineteen years old I found myself with a new opportunity to reinvent myself, and I took it with open arms. I was moving to a completely new part of the country, and I was going to university.

> *My parents said "goodbye", and I found myself alone, sitting on my bed feeling absolutely dumbfounded. I had no idea what I had just done – my life would never be the same again, and I had no idea how I would cope with this massive change I had just made.*
>
> *I had officially left home, and I felt small, scared, and pretty much frozen.*
>
> *I didn't know how I would ever leave this room I had somehow found myself in, but if I stayed in here I didn't know how I might cope. My room resembled how I would expect a jail cell to look. It was possibly a nice jail cell, but my walls were painted concrete blocks, bare and uninspiring. My parents had made a start with me, but they had left me to figure out how I wanted my room to look. I didn't know where to start. My instinct was to run, but I could hear people everywhere chatting, laughing, unpacking, organizing. Some people were meeting and getting to know each other; others were saying goodbye. Everyone sounded so sociable, confident, and assured.*
>
> *I felt alone.*
>
> *I was absolutely terrified.*
>
> *There were just so many people, so many strangers. I don't know if I would have ever made a move if there hadn't just then been a knock at my door.*

In my days at university, many things changed. I

travelled during my holidays and had some amazing experiences. I worked hard and I played even harder. I kept myself busy – too busy to notice that my insecurities remained. I thought if I ignored them, they would eventually go away. I decided that if I kept moving away from them, I would become this other person, magically fun and engaging.

On the one hand I was creating goals and dreams for myself. I was planning to travel extensively, and I was imagining a life of adventure. I had no desire to follow the urge other people were having to find a job and settle down. I wanted to go out into the world and see what else life had in store for me. I was still regarded as quiet by many, but I was no longer painfully so.

If I stopped here, I knew what would happen. I would never become more than I was. I would always remain with the 'quiet' stigma hanging over my head.

I needed to move again, and I needed to move further away. I needed another fresh start. I needed another opportunity to reinvent myself – and to finally release myself from the struggles of my past.

The plan was that my best friend Kim and I would travel through Southeast Asia and find ourselves in New Zealand two months later. Life would be fun, exciting, and full.

And it was.

I continued with my work-hard, play-hard ethic from university, and for a while I was having the time of my life. I pushed all of my insecurities away when they arose, and so I didn't see that I was heading for a crash.

When it came, it hit me hard. I was becoming more and more emotional when I was drinking, and after the first six months in Wanaka, I was a bit of a wreck. Somehow this was also the time that I met my current partner, Simon. A relationship was the last thing I wanted at the time, but the stability helped me to begin releasing the flood of emotions I had been holding back, and something about our meeting simply felt right.

I began to experience night terrors, and night by night my fears, struggles, and insecurities were screamed out of me as I slept. Simon was always there – frustrated at times – but he never doubted that one day I would shine. I'm not sure he would have stayed if he knew how long it might take – but lucky for us both he did!

My struggles at that time came from the burgeoning realization that I had run out of options. I had run as far as I possibly could. Here I was on the other side of the world, and despite Simon, my life seemed to be falling apart. This was not how it was supposed to be!

To begin with I had tried to fit in at school by pretending that I could speak just like everybody else. Unsatisfied with my attempts, I tried again at a college in a new town. University was another opportunity to cast off my old stigma and reinvent myself, and finally when I came to New Zealand, I was giving myself the biggest push away from my pain.

I didn't realize that the very thing I had been running from for so long would turn out to be the one thing that I wanted more than anything else in my life. It took me a long time to see the irony – I had been running from myself for all those years.

Now I can look back and see why I was falling apart after those first few months in this country. I knew that this was it. I didn't have anywhere else to run; New Zealand was as far away as I could possibly get. I was starting to realize that despite all of my efforts, I was still fundamentally the same. I was still me, underneath all of my attempts to change that, and I still felt quiet. I still felt wrong.

When I came to New Zealand and didn't magically feel cured, I had begun to realize that I would have to face the very thing that I had avoided for my whole life.

I would have to come face to face with myself.

13. Life doesn't have to be a battle

There's nothing like a challenge to set you back on track ...

Have you ever looked into your own eyes? Looking at yourself in the mirror – and truly seeing the person who looks back - is possibly the most difficult thing in the world to do. It is easy to run around, finding distractions, and avoiding those parts of life that cause you discomfort or pain, but at some point it becomes necessary for most of us to move away from the comfort zone – and start walking the path of truly figuring out who we are.

For some people it comes as an illness. Some people are faced with sudden loss or an accident that changes an aspect of their lives. For me it came when I slept.

I was working as the manager of a restaurant at the time, and we had been advertising on one of the local radio stations. As a 'Thank you!' for our advertising dollars, we were shouted a trip to Doubtful Sound with a bunch of other local businesses.

My boss nominated me to go.

Two nights in Doubtful Sound is an idyllic-sounding retreat from life. We were staying on a fishing boat, and our sleeping quarters were pretty cramped. I saw them and at once became scared.

My fears were acknowledged the next day as I woke up to,

"Who was that screaming last night?"

I was mortified. Night terrors had become a nightly occurrence for me over the past few years, but when I was at home it was one thing. Sleeping on a boat full of strangers – and waking them all up with my piercing screams and overzealous attempts to save my life was more than I was ready to deal with.

I spent most of that second day in shock, wishing I could somehow disappear. I didn't want this anymore, and so when I returned home I began to do some research.

Everywhere I looked it said the same thing. Adult on-set night terrors were extremely rare and believed to be incurable. Like it or not, this was me for the rest of my days.

On the one hand I was elated to find that I was suffering from a named condition – and that I wasn't losing my mind. On the other hand, I was pretty upset by my prognosis.

I would never again feel comfortable staying over at other people's houses. I would not accept another offer to go on a free overnight trip in a beautiful part of the world.

I would avoid staying in backpackers or going camping …

Every night I walked into battle. I fought off avalanches; I pushed apart caves; I struggled to turn the car away from the cliff's edge; I frantically searched for the magic button that would prevent the bomb from exploding … there are so many scenarios. At the end of each one I would awaken, the room pounding with every beat of my heart, my whole body shaking, sometimes in spasms, as I cowered in confusion, waiting to die.

I imagined myself as an old lady, still screaming the house down every night. I feared for how my body might cope with so much adrenaline pouring through my aging body. I struggled to accept it, and something clicked.

I wasn't going to accept this in my life.

Night terrors might have been announced as incurable, but they weren't going to remain with me for the rest of my life. I would try a different approach. I would fight them. I would do whatever it took – and I would overcome this nightly battle.

I reclaimed my power in that moment, and my life since then has been a difficult and extremely fulfilling return to my truth.

To begin with I visited my doctor. I was quite disturbed by the twitching of her lip as I described what I was going through. The way she pulled her smile down at one side, so it didn't look like she was amused. I wasn't too worried, though; I knew how ridiculous it must sound, and she had not come across night terrors in adults before. After mumbling something about various forms of medication and why they wouldn't really be appropriate, I was officially pronounced incurable – and we hadn't even tried anything yet.

I certainly wasn't going to settle for that!

I took it upon myself to find a way through. This was different than my childhood when I had been able to find ways to push away my feelings and avoid situations that heightened my anxiety. Night terrors would happen whether I wanted them to or not – because they happened when I was asleep. I had no conscious method of controlling their occurrence. I had no choice now but to face myself.

To begin with, I tried various forms of therapy.

- **Hypnotherapy** (helped a little, particularly self-hypnosis at bedtime)
- **Craniosacral therapy** (a little bit more, and it's oh so relaxing!)
- **Acupuncture** (pushed me a touch further)
- **Rebirthing** (intense, but fascinating and very helpful)
- **Reiki** (also intense for the attunements, and wonderful for the treatments)
- **Kinesiology** (really, really interesting)
- **Meditation** (hit and miss, but I keep coming back to it)

... and so much more. The thing I noticed with every practitioner that I visited was that the bit I enjoyed the most was the talking bit. Talking to a professional was different than talking to other people. I felt safe and important. I felt like there was never any pressure – and I slowly realized that when I spoke in this kind of situation I was speaking from a place that had long desired to have its voice heard.

I was speaking from my heart.

I was speaking from my needs.

I was speaking in a way that had always needed to be heard so that I could work my way past the challenges I had in my life.

I had no idea at the time that all of this was so relevant to my childhood issues with selective mutism, but now I see that it was how I began to reconnect with the place inside of me that had always longed to have its say.

The ball of words and emotions that had collected inside of my throat was finally unraveling. Between the night terrors and the therapies I chose to relieve my night terror symptoms – I was overcoming something that I had forgotten needed my attention. I was finding a way to unwind my selective mutism symptoms that still remained. I was taking steps back toward the little girl who had once so desperately wanted to share herself, but had no idea how to do it in this world.

14. Finding my Voice

There is little in my life that brings me more joy than being able to connect with and speak my own words!

Somewhere between my first hypnotherapy session and today, I have experienced some monumental shifts in my life. My sense of self, my health, and my ability to speak with my own voice have been through some huge transformations.

I hadn't realized, but up until about eight or ten years ago, the voice I used to speak was still the pretend voice I had adopted when I was about seven years old. There was a subtle forcefulness to it – as though I was speaking because I felt like I should rather than because I wanted to. The origin of this voice was shallow and felt like it came from the top part of my throat. When I spoke with this voice, it was always from a place of seeking acceptance and hoping to meet expectations. It was the part of me that craved normality and hoped to be seen as being 'just like everybody else'.

My true voice emerged gradually. I first heard it

when I began to visit the various therapists while I was hoping to find a cure for my night terrors. I noticed that I felt relaxed talking about myself and my desires in this setting. Looking back now I can see that this was because these people had no expectations of me. I was paying for therapy, and these professionals would accept me no matter how I presented to them.

I spent a lot of hours in this past decade 'working on my stuff'. This means that I have gradually, at a pace that I felt comfortable with, come face to face with myself. I guess, in a way, it is quite like the 'Sliding In' technique that I mentioned in chapter 4. Just like the protocol for children, I started to gently expand my comfort zone, introducing new aspects when I felt ready to. When I began the process, I suffered from night terrors several times each night and was wrought with insecurities and a huge amount of suppressed anxiety. In contrast, today I am feeling considerably freer and capable of coping with many more situations in an authentic way.

It is hugely important to me that I feel like myself as I move through my life. I am so acutely aware of other people and the things they are thinking and feeling that it can be easy to fall off balance and lean toward my old habits and their expectations. However, whenever I do, I notice that the flow of my life decreases and things just seem to become more difficult.

One day, when I was thirty-one, I was suffering a mild panic attack at home when I felt an uncontrollable urge to say something. The words I used were incomprehensible to me, and they came out fluently and powerfully, in a voice that did not sound like the one I was used to hearing. I felt like I was speaking a combination of several languages - none of which I could physically understand, but in some crazy way they were able to express exactly what I was feeling. From that moment on I found that whenever I was feeling emotionally overwhelmed, this 'gibberish' speak would help me to release my feelings and move past them.

Gradually I became more comfortable speaking like this to release my feelings - I only did it when I was by myself - and something happened inside of me. I became aware that I didn't feel so tense, and I didn't find it so difficult to express myself as I was used to. Situations sometimes made me jump, and I would let out an involuntary "yelp" to express my surprise. This freedom of expression was new to me. I was a little scared of what might fall out of my mouth, but in the same way as I had struggled to say anything as a child, my anxiety about looking a little bit crazy held me back from reacting in this way in any situation where I felt discomfort.

My young daughter and I made a game out of talking in made-up languages. She was three at the time, and when we played our game, I felt more connected to both my daughter and myself than I had for a long time.

It was really interesting to notice around this time that my voice, when I was talking normally, started to take on a different quality. It was as though I had connected with the part of me that I had suppressed for years. My voice came from deep inside of me instead of the top of my throat, and I felt like I was finally able to communicate my truth.

It has been amazing to reconnect with my voice. Today I notice an excitement that grows inside of me each time I realise that I have something to say. This development of words, opinions, ideas, and arguments bubbles from inside of me, and I can recognise its energy as my own.

It has always been a dream of mine to speak from this place of passion and purpose, to share my thoughts and ideas, and to be open about my opinions.

Since my voice first began to emerge I have noticed a deep sense of fulfilment that grows with each new situation that I am able to speak in.

About five years ago, I began to connect with my passion for communication. It shocked me because I had always thought that communication was one of my weaknesses. However, when I considered it I realised that I probably knew more about communication than most.

For many years, verbal communication felt forced and difficult to me, but I think this was because of the extreme awareness that I had about words and their origins. The words a person speaks only tell part of the story, and I was accustomed to listening with my eyes more than my ears. I have always been aware of the subtle communication that people use all the time, even when we are not speaking, the subtle changes in our expressions and gestures that indicate a particular thought pattern or emotional trigger. It has never been so much what was said, but the way it was spoken that resonated with me. If the words and gestures did not match I would always pick it up. I think this is something that everyone is aware of, whether we are conscious of it or not, and this is why some people come across as genuine while other people make us wary.

Words are simply the topmost layer of something that begins with a motivation to communicate.

A little like Chinese whispers, by the time communication works its way up from our intention, through our thoughts and emotions, into our expressions and gestures and then out of our mouth, the words we use can sometimes struggle to truly convey exactly what we hoped that they would. Have you ever struggled to find the word that is the best fit for your explanation? Did you ever say something and it came out wrong? Do you sometimes feel the need to stop for a moment so you can craft your sentence in the way you want it to sound?

I have come to the understanding that when someone comes across as truly authentic in the way that they speak, it is because their words match the original intention of what they wanted to say.

> *Five years ago I joined Toastmasters. I knew very little about the public speaking club, but I felt drawn to it because I believed it would help me to overcome the limitations I still had around speaking.*
>
> *My first meeting was terrifying. I shivered and sweated my way through my first ninety seconds of public speaking, and then I put up my hand to deliver my 'Icebreaker' speech at the following meeting. I knew if I didn't volunteer there was little chance of me going back, and I really wanted to overcome this fear.*
>
> *For the first two years, I would go to every meeting a bundle of nerves. I would sit in my seat shaking, as I waited for my turn to speak – and after it was over the relief would flood me with emotion so huge I would often return home in floods of tears.*
>
> *I am now the president of our club. I have spoken in many different settings. I feel comfortable enough to stand up wherever I am and no matter how many people I am faced with and share my thoughts. Public speaking is something that feels quite natural to me today.*

I attribute Toastmasters as being a major boost to both my confidence and speaking ability. When I first joined, I would struggle to convey what I wanted to. I would lose my train of thought and trip up around words. I spoke quickly, without breathing, and would leave the stage feeling overwhelmed with no idea of what had just happened or anything that I said. The supportive environment helped me to feel comfortable enough to relax enough to gather my thoughts. I have grown to be able to trust that, no matter what, I can stand up and say something genuine.

Two years ago, I attended a conference. On the first day I sat back and listened, but on day two I felt compelled to stand up and share my thoughts. The interesting thing was, as I stood up to speak, all I knew was that I had something that I wanted to say. I didn't even know what it was.

This experience was about trusting myself and this new connection to my voice. In a room full of about one hundred people, I started speaking and surprised myself with the clarity and message of my words. Nothing has ever felt so good as speaking at this conference – with no preparation, just a strong conviction that I had something to offer and trusting that my words would fit.

In this chapter I have talked a lot about my speaking voice, but in truth our voice is so much more than the words that we speak.

From childhood I have adored drawing and writing as vehicles of expression and communication. When all other doors were closed to me, I could always draw a picture. Whether people gleaned meaning from the things that I drew didn't really matter – the main thing was that I was able to draw freely, and my work was always appreciated.

Today I love to communicate visually through

graphic design and illustration. Colours and shapes communicate their own messages, and of course, there is the old saying that 'a picture says a thousand words'. I used to think about this and wish that I could actually speak a thousand words, but today I can appreciate the tremendous capability of art, photography, and other forms of visual communication to say the things that often words struggle to accurately convey.

We all have a creative voice, whether we are aware of it or not. Our particular vehicle may be art, design, photography, or it may be dance, drama, or music. It may even be speaking – and the ability to entertain with your words. Some people believe that they 'do not have a creative bone in their body', but I don't believe this is true. I think that we all have our own unique, creative voice. Perhaps your artwork was not appreciated as a child, and so you grew up believing that you could not draw. In truth, we all have our own style; it's just that some of these stand out as talent, and others are dismissed. It doesn't mean their creator was not creative, and it doesn't mean that they can't draw, dance, sing, or speak.

15. Two steps forward

Sometimes we need to take one step back ...

There was a time that I thought life flowed in a straight line. I believed that when I overcame one obstacle it would forever remain behind me, and I would move forward toward whatever came next. I thought that if something suddenly became easier for me one day, I would always find it easy.

Unfortunately, this mind-set made it very difficult for me to cope when I found myself facing circumstances and emotional reactions that I had been through before – and it was especially difficult to revisit behaviour patterns that I thought I had left behind long ago.

> *As a thirty one year old Mum I had only recently found out about selective mutism, but I believed that its manifestation in my life remained safely tucked away in the past. One day I was playing with both of my kids when my almost two-year-old son jumped on my tummy (hard!!).*
>
> *My first reaction was to let out a yelp, but as I attempted to explain to his shocked reaction that I was okay I was shocked to find that I was only able to whisper. My (then three-year-old) daughter was intrigued and asked me question after question. No matter how hard she tried, she couldn't draw out*

my normal voice.

I was becoming frustrated with all this questioning, so in a moment of possible madness I suggested we could go to the park instead. In hindsight, taking two pre-schoolers and a dog to the park in an attempt to rediscover my voice was probably not the wisest move I've ever made.

While we were there I was constantly running after the kids when I needed to talk to them, making sure they stayed close. I didn't dare let our dog run around with no voice to call him back, so he stayed close too. As we were getting ready to leave I noticed a group of young men pointing towards us. I froze as I realised that they were walking our way, and shuddered as one of them looked straight into my eyes and asked,

"Is this your dog?"

I sucked in my cheek as I struggled with my desire to say something so he might leave, and my fear that if I did manage it he might ask me more questions. Experience had shown me that there were certain people who loved boxers, and these people could keep us in conversation for hours if I let them. I opened my mouth, thinking it might help if I did start a conversation, but I couldn't make a sound. I closed my mouth again and nodded, as I looked down and gave a lop-sided shy smile, then I patted the kids shoulders and motioned for them to start walking back to the car. I was mortified!

This experience shocked me ... I had thought of selective mutism as being a thing of the past – it was something I had believed to have overcome a long time ago. What I began to discover on that day was that the potential for selective mutism is something that comes along with my temperament, and is not something that will probably ever truly go away.

High sensitivity and a tendency toward overwhelm when I'm over stimulated can very easily trigger anxiety. Unmanaged anxiety can increase and when it does I occasionally still exhibit symptoms of selective mutism. The last time was only a few months ago – which makes me question any approach or desire to *overcome* selective mutism.

Perhaps 'overcome' is the wrong word to use. In my opinion, by working to overcome or fight our potential for selective mutism we are in turn working against who we are. To my mind, this does not mean that we have to accept the fact that we will never be able to talk like everybody else, but it also doesn't mean that we have to continually push the boundaries of our comfort zone so that we can.

Working with selective mutism means that we look for ways to acknowledge and accept our sensitive personalities – giving ourselves the time and space that we need to adjust to situations that cause anxiety, as well as the reassurance that we are already perfect versions of ourselves.

In this way, any symptom of selective mutism becomes an indication that we have pushed ourselves too far. Selective mutism becomes the communication that tells us when we need to slow down, retreat and re-connect with who we are. We were not made to be like 'everybody else', we were made in our own unique way. People with selective mutism have a huge amount to offer the world, but if we are to find a way to share this we need to notice and acknowledge our value. We need to realise that there are certain environments that are extremely challenging for us to function in, but there are other environments within which we can thrive.

16. If I could turn back time

To my parents, my teachers, and my younger self ...

If I could go back to my early years now, I would love to be able to help my parents, my teachers, and myself to understand what we were all going through and to give each of us a few insights to hold on to. With all I have learnt through each experience I have had, it is my hope that it can have some far-reaching effects. I believe that I am the person I am today because of the difficulties I once faced.

If you are reading this book I can imagine you may have some connection to selective mutism. Perhaps you are the parent of someone who suffers, or maybe you suffer yourself. Or you could be a teacher, a therapist, a friend, or family member ... The words that follow come from me, in relation to my experience, but I hope they offer some comfort and direction for your own personal journey.

First and foremost, I would ask my parents not to

worry ... the amazing little girl they know may not share herself as openly as everyone would like, but she will not always be this way.

Life has a way of teaching us the things we need to grow in the most interesting ways, and time can only tell how much we all have to learn from my selective mutism.

I would ask my parents not to question the way I am, but to accept and love me for it. Beneath the selectively mute traits that I exhibit lies a gentle sensitivity; a caring nature; an inquisitive, creative spark; and so much more. These are the things they need to notice and nurture, not the way I present myself to the world. Given time, acceptance, and a whole lot of love, the way I talk and share myself will expand.

Please, take the energy you spend worrying about my future and apply it instead to noticing how much I already have to offer.

Most of all, I would ask my parents to give themselves credit for all they do as a mum and a dad. Nothing is more important than their belief that they are doing the best that they can, and to feel good about the way they have helped my brother and me to navigate our early years. We pick up on their feelings, and our sensitive natures will translate these into our developing belief systems. We need to know that we are okay. We need to know that our parents believe in us exactly the way that we are.

Meeting my teachers, I would answer the question I heard too many times as a young child. I would tell them that I am aware that some of them asked out of concern, and some asked out of frustration, but I would let them know that regardless of their reasons, questioning me was always going to be the least effective way to get me to open up.

I would explain that I was quiet because I suffered from selective mutism, and I was suffering from levels of anxiety that were so huge I literally couldn't say a word in situations outside of my home. This anxiety became exacerbated by the reactions of the people around me, and the approach of my teachers played a huge role in helping me feel either more or less comfortable. I would ask them to become aware of the part they play in reducing or increasing my anxiety levels, and to start looking for ways that they may be able to help to reduce those feelings for me.

I would ask that teachers do not show that they notice when more or less communication is used, and I would ask that they acknowledge all non-verbal communication as though it was spoken out loud.

I would also point out that many children suffer from anxiety at various levels, and all of these children have strengths and talents that they may have difficulty sharing. I would stress the need for empathy in the classroom, and teaching styles that value listening and thinking as much as they value participation.

I would suggest that perhaps the opportunity to spend some time in a small room with less stimulation might help - a place where more sensitive children might go to wind down and recharge. Maybe we could figure out a way to make sure children like me always make it to the toilet. I would stress the importance of educating all teachers, and when necessary sourcing additional help such as a teacher aide. In addition I would share the 'sliding in' technique, and encourage teachers to realize that by adopting a more sensitive teaching style they may literally turn the future of children such as me around by helping us to feel accepted, heard and worthy.

Lastly, if I were to meet my younger self today I would be immediately filled with love and awe for all she is. I would encourage her to always stay true to herself.

I would make sure that she understands the importance of these words – I would ask her to only speak when she is able to use her own words, and to not feel pressured into talking because other people want or expect it.

I would tell her that it doesn't matter if she can't speak a lot right now; the words she wants to say will come out another time, in another place, when they are ready to be spoken, and equally as importantly, when they are ready to be heard.

I would tell her that I love her. I love her exactly the way she is – and I would ask that she remain her beautiful self no matter what other people demand that she become.

After that, I would cry for the more difficult road that I travelled, and I would hope that she chooses to take the easier route.

I hope you are able to understand that you have much to offer the world, whether you are capable of speaking to it or not. In part two, my purpose is to remind each of us how incredible we are, regardless of anything we cannot do. I hope it will help you to recognise and embrace your talents and empower you to share your own unique wonder with the world.

Part Two

Beyond Selective Mutism

Peeling back the labels of selective mutism, quietness, and shyness, I have discovered an incredible range of talents and traits that deserve celebration ...

People with selective mutism are talented artists, writers, singers, gymnasts, athletes, scientists, teachers, parents, and so much more. We have a huge amount to offer and share through our **intelligent, sensitive, creative personalities** – but sometimes we get lost inside of our behavior, and we forget how to be ourselves.

> **"You're the Voice,**
> **try and understand it,**
> **Make a noise and make it**
> **clear ... "**
>
> John Farnham, "You're the Voice"

Whether you can speak or not, you have a voice that you use every day. You can choose to hide that voice and feel powerless over your own life, or you can use it in your own unique way and make your mark on the world.

17. You're the Voice

Overcoming selective mutism can be a demanding, consuming journey – but are we forgetting what we already have?

Our voices are interesting things. Sometimes we choose when and how to use them, and other times they seem to choose when and how to use us. Our voices expand from the words we use into the way that we speak, the tone of our voice, the speed with which we talk, the things we will share and the things we choose to leave out. Our voices also speak when we cannot. They speak through our silence. In fact, they speak through everything we do …

Our voices arise with the first spark of intention and speak through the ways that we move, our gestures, actions, and inactions, the clothes that we wear, the choices we make, the choices we let other people make for us. We are speaking through our likes and our dislikes, our hopes and our dreams, our sadness and our fears. Whatever we are holding back tells a story, just as when we stand up and talk about every intricacy of whatever we are choosing to share - who we will open up to, and whom we will not, the reactions of others, and whether that encourages us to retreat, attack, or embrace.

Our voices are present in the things that we like, the games that we play ... in everything that we do and everything that we don't do. We say as much with our creativity as with our difficulty, whether we move with flexibility or with stiffness, whether we have a lot to say or a little or nothing at all.

My point is, whether you are capable of speaking or not, you have a voice that you are using all the time.

People are responding to your voice ... and your voice responds to them. This response may or may not involve words. It may or may not involve speech. If your voice is authentic and reflects who you are and the best choices that you can make in this moment, then is this not a cause for celebration?

I am not a person who likes to dwell on things, and I don't really regret, for I believe that I have only ever made the best choices I was capable of making at the time. However, if I could go back into the past and change one thing, I would make sure that I do not talk until I am ready to use my own words. I would focus on reducing my anxiety instead of caving in to the pressure to say something. I would be myself and I would not try to fit in.

Hindsight is a wonderful thing ... but doing things the way I have has led me to the perspective that I am happy to have today. I believe that the challenges we face in our lives are there for a reason. I think of them as directions, showing us the best and most fulfilling ways to grow. Sometimes it can take a long time to notice the way life is trying to direct us, and often it can seem to be in a direction we'd rather not go, but eventually we get to look back with gratitude for the lessons our life situations have been able to teach us.

I feel hugely lucky to have lived the life I have, and am, living. Without selective mutism, I think I would be living a life lacking the depth and understanding that I now enjoy. I would not have suffered so much, but I would not have gained as much either. I think this is the gift that any difficulty holds inside, and this is what I would like to explore in the following chapters.

What is it about people who suffer from selective mutism that deserves celebration? What are our unique gifts?

More specifically, what is your unique gift? Why were you created the way you are, and how can you embrace this so that you can move past your fears and offer it to the world?

18. Working with selective mutism

Developing a strong sense of self ...

Selective mutism is a condition that appears when triggered in susceptible individuals. In this way it could be seen to be a part of the sufferer's potential ... a set of symptoms that serve to indicate when the way we are living our life is not in alignment with our needs.

People who exhibit these symptoms are usually said to be bright, intelligent, creative individuals – and we are also sensitive, intuitive, and empathic. Our sensitive side is one that is often overlooked or may be seen as a difficulty, but it is an intrinsic part of who we are. If you ask me, this part of us needs to be acknowledged, accepted and worked with so we can share our goodness with the world.

I believe that the potential for selective mutism will always remain in people like me, regardless of whether we continue to experience its symptoms within our lives. I also think that the definition of 'overcoming' is a difficult one to define, as it can mean something different depending upon your perspective. However, I do believe that if we are able to find a way of living our lives that is balanced and appreciative of our needs then we can live free from the symptoms of selective mutism.

Going from my own experience, I think one of the most important things to develop for the sufferer of selective mutism is your sense of self. At home you probably feel comfortable enough to be yourself most of the time, but if something changes, (like a new person coming over, or you go somewhere new) suddenly you become thrown off balance, and you lose a bit of your certainty. You feel like you have lost your centre and you struggle to reclaim it as your anxiety levels rise.

I think it is important to become aware of your boundaries: Where do you end? Where do other people begin? Do you ever walk into a room full of people and find yourself completely overwhelmed? No matter how you felt in the moment before you stepped through that door, everything suddenly changed when your energy mixed with the energy of the room. Suddenly you might not feel like yourself anymore – and so you have no idea of how to act, or what to do. You literally feel paralysed as your anxiety rises and panic sets in.

You need an anchor to remind you of who you are, because at the moment you feel like a tiny rowing boat in a very large, stormy ocean.

This ability to sense other people is what makes you the caring, thoughtful, empathic person you are. However, it can also be your undoing if you aren't aware that this is happening.

You may feel like the floor has been taken from under you as you become swept away in the goings on of everybody else. This is where you need to stop and re-group – to take some conscious breaths, and remind yourself of who you are – or have someone to help you with this. It's a bit like giving that tiny rowing boat an anchor, so it can't get swept away. There is nothing more important to me than remembering who I am in every situation I find myself in. The more I do this, the easier it becomes, and so my sense of self grows too.

Whenever I find it necessary to stop and re-group, there are certain things that help me. You might find different ways to cope, but I will share what works for me here ...

I always tune in to my breath.

My breath reminds me that I am my own person, and I am here living this life that flows through me. I find it calming to notice how I am breathing, and then to consciously work to slow my breathing down. I recently took a buteyko course, and was shocked to learn that the deep breaths I had often used in an attempt to quell my anxiety were actually exacerbating it. Over-breathing can very easily trigger anxiety, so slowing your breathing down and making sure each breath is making use of the diaphragm is actually a very effective way to relieve your symptoms.

I notice my body

Looking at my hands is something I often do to stop anxiety in its tracks. I always find myself mesmerised a little by the realisation that 'these are my hands!' as I move my fingers and notice my own unique markings on my skin.

Another thing I sometimes do is to look at myself in the mirror. I am suddenly clearly defined as the person looking back, and I realise that I am actually much smaller than all those big feelings that threaten to engulf me.

I love myself

When I first tried doing this, I found it impossible. Saying those three simple words to myself was incredibly difficult. "I love you" were three words that brought with them unprecedented emotion, and because they brought so much emotion I realised how important they were. After all, if we can't love ourselves, how can we expect anyone else to love us?

Some people recommend standing in front of a mirror and saying "I love you" out loud – and while I agree that this is incredibly powerful, I started much smaller than this. I would lie in bed and as I fell asleep I'd dare myself to think it. It took me a while to work up to actually thinking "I love you" and then even longer before I felt like I meant it. Now I say it to myself as often as I remember, and I find it helps to remind myself of this when I am feeling anxious or scared.

I meet my needs

I believe that our feelings play a very important role in our lives. In a way they are the directors – showing us who we are beyond the realms of who we think we are, or who we think we should be. Our feelings can often surprise us, as we react more or less strongly to a set of stimuli than we thought we might, and they also serve to remind us of our needs.

Our feelings let us know when we are hungry, or when we have eaten too much. They indicate when something is good for us, or when something might be a bad idea.

Nothing has made such a profound difference in my life than when I started to listen to my feelings, and what they were trying to tell me. I started to eat better, to go with what felt good and to steer away from what felt bad.

In turn, I gained more trust in myself and my ability to understand and meet my needs. I started to drop unhealthy habits and adopt new, more healthy ones. I became much more empowered, and I realized that I felt much more confident too. I began to realize that I matter more to me than anyone else on this planet, and that understanding helped me to move my life in a direction that has been exciting and hugely fulfilling.

19. Freedom from expectation

Choosing to speak because there is something we want to say and long to share ...

Whenever we interact with people, we are learning a little bit about them. What is it that makes these people tick? How do they think? How much do they share, and what do they expect from others?

What do they expect from you? What do you expect from them?

Having spent a large portion of my life being motivated largely by the pressure I felt to meet the expectations of other people, I have a few words to say about the potentially damaging effect that expectations can have, as well as the freedom that we can feel when there are no expectations put upon us.

Living up to expectations can be a tricky business. I have always associated expectations with pressure, and also with anxiety. I think that a person's sensitivity can have a lot to do with whether we notice expectations or not, and also whether it matters to us if we meet them or not. This, and the strength of our own sense of self ... the more that we know who we are, and feel strong enough to stay true to that, the less likely we are to be swayed by the wants, needs, and expectations of another.

The expectation to speak within the society that we live is a massive one. When a person asks another person a question, they are usually expecting an answer, or at least a response. Often, they will have a feeling about what that response might be – maybe based upon previous experiences with the person or whatever they are hoping to hear. They might also have a feeling about their preferred response. This feeling they are having is their expectation. An expectation is not something that needs to be met, but it is something that some people are quite attached to.

Speaking from my own experience, I can say that the expectations of a person when they talk to somebody with selective mutism can literally make all the difference within the interaction.

It is the difference between asking a closed question and waiting for the answer, to asking an open, inviting question that is more rhetorical than demanding of an answer.

The way a question is framed and the motivations behind it can literally make a world of difference to the person with selective mutism. If the person asking has a strong expectation, and is attached to that particular outcome, the person being asked may feel a certain amount of pressure to conform and meet those expectations. This is where people with selective mutism are likely to struggle the most. If, however, the person asking the question is unattached to any particular outcome, that pressure will be released. A person with selective mutism will notice that there is no pressure to speak.

Pressure is instantly relieved when there is no perceived expectation to speak, and at the same time, the anxieties ease a little too. It is in this scenario that someone who suffers from selective mutism might make some headway – because suddenly they might find that they are able to make a choice about whether they would like to speak, or not. The other person has shown that it does not matter whether they reply or not, and in this way it is instantly more easy to reply. There is no expectation to meet.

There is, however, an added dimension that might become an additional issue – and this happens when people stop expecting the person with selective mutism to speak. It is very easy for us to meet this expectation, and even when our anxiety levels lessen, we then find it difficult to talk because that becomes what is expected of us. Rising above expectations is therefore an important skill to learn.

I think it is important to help children to develop their sense of self, and in doing so, to ease the pressure that expectations can so easily create. It is equally important for adults to develop their sense of self too. When somebody feels completely happy inside of themself, it will not matter to them if they do not meet the expectations of another.

As I have gained strength within my own sense of self, I have been able to realize that every interaction can be the open-ended, expectation-free interaction if you want it to be. I have been able to see that whether I reply to a person's question or not is my decision to make. Their expectation belongs to them, and it is not up to me to meet that – it is up to me to respond in my own, unique way. Sometimes, this might involve an answer, and sometimes it might not ... the point is that this kind of response comes because of me and not because of them.

How important is it to you to meet the expectations that other people hold? How much anxiety does this create? Do you find that it sometimes feels more important to please others than to feel happy and comfortable within yourself?

One of the biggest lessons of my life has been the importance of living for myself. It has taken me years to reach this place, and occasionally I still feel the pull of expectation. Most of the time I speak because I want to, not because other people expect it from me, and the same goes for the things I do in my life. In my opinion, there is nothing better than speaking up because you have something to say, or doing something because it lights you up inside ...

20. Celebrate your talents!

At the core of who we are we each have our own unique impulses, desires, passions, and talents ...

I have spent a large portion of my life noticing the parts of me that I didn't like. It felt very easy to notice that I wanted to change; I wanted to be able to talk like other people; I wanted to come across as friendly and easygoing and fun.

The more that I focused on my difficulties, the more importance I gave them. What had begun when I was small as something that had a relatively insignificant impact upon my experience of life gradually became an all-consuming problem that I longed to change no matter what the cost. Speaking freely was the one thing I longed to experience.

Unfortunately, it was also the thing I found most difficult to do ... and so, I spent much of my life feeling like a failure.

Regardless of my perception, there were many, many things that I was good at. I was creative and very talented at drawing, painting, and making things. I loved to write too, and my short stories and poems often found praise. I was intelligent and could think both creatively and logically.

I was flexible and fit, and I enjoyed gymnastics outside of school. I remember stretching myself effortlessly into many different poses and smiling to myself as I watched other people struggle to achieve anything even remotely close.

There were many things that I was good at, and I haven't even begun to explore my temperament and the related treasures that were hidden away behind my tendency toward quiet.

I have always had many talents, but unfortunately, they were almost all overshadowed by the one thing that I struggled with the most.

The fact that I suffered from selective mutism kept me feeling small. I am all for modesty, but when I think about it honestly, it shocks me to realize how much I have held myself back in life, how many of my choices were made out of fear, and the resulting things I did not do.

It hurts me to think of the number of people who also hold themselves and their talents back because of their difficulties with selective mutism, all of the people who feel that, in some way, life does not have a place for them because they cannot talk and say what they long to say. Their physical voice is missing, and somehow they forget that they are speaking all the time through the things that they do and the choices they make.

How might our world look if people with selective mutism were completely accepted with or without speech? How might your world look, or the world of your child, if it didn't matter whether you were speaking or not?

In my opinion, everybody has some things they are good at and some things that they are not so good at. We all have a particular set of talents that, were we to embrace them, would help to light up the world. We each have a choice whether to pursue those things that we excel at or to dwell on the things that hold us back.

Speech is a difficult struggle to have because there are so many expectations surrounding it within society. There is a general expectation that as people we will speak to communicate, just as we read and write. If we struggle with any of these fundamental skills, then our perceived value in life might be questioned.

I would like to live in a world where none of this really matters. Whether we can speak, read, write, or not makes little difference to the person we are inside – the person we are at the very core of our being. At our centre, we each have impulses and desires. We each have motivations in our own unique direction, and we each have our own talents that we could choose to share with the world.

In my opinion, people are celebrated when they shrug off any adversity they face and pursue their talents and passions regardless. They plunge themselves into whatever it is that lights them up inside, and they do that thing whenever they can, until eventually that thing becomes an intrinsic part of who they are. It does not matter to their particular talent that they cannot do this other thing.

Not one person was made to do everything in life ... it is our different impulses, dreams, desires, passions, and talents that make the world such an interesting place to be.

If I could request just one thing of you, it would be that you focus on your strengths, your talents, and the things that make you light up inside. If you don't know what they are, then maybe you could just reach toward something that makes you feel a little better than the way you are feeling now. The nature of life is that it is a constantly moving, changing web of experience. The thing that we think we will end up doing becomes a steppingstone toward something more when we simply pursue whatever it is that makes us feel good.

Feeling good is something that everybody deserves in life, and we can all feel good if we choose to move in that direction. Look at the thing that you would do right now if nothing else mattered, and then do that thing as often as you are able ... and see where it takes you.

21. Set some attainable goals

The greatest journey begins with a single step ...

When I was a child, I knew exactly what I wanted to achieve in my life. I wanted to be normal, and I wanted to be able to speak freely in all situations.

Normal was my ultimate goal, and I was prepared to do many things to reach it. However, normal is elusive and difficult to achieve for the reason that its definition depends upon your perspective. The closer you get to achieving your realms of normal, the more those realms are likely to morph, change, and expand – until suddenly you appear to have taken several steps back instead of forward.

A goal such as "I just want to be normal!" or "I want to overcome selective mutism" or "I want to be better" is, in my opinion, incredibly difficult to ever achieve. *How will you know when you finally reach it?*

I guess the biggest clue will come when you no longer have the desire to reach your particular goal. For the purposes of overcoming a condition that has kept you playing small and feeling 'less than' for the majority of your life, the likelihood is that unless you change your approach you will probably never reach it. And if you actually do, what will you aim for then?

As people, we attract energy towards us by the strength of our desires. Have you ever woken up hugely excited about a particular thing you will do on that day? You jump out of bed much more easily than usual and feel like you have endless energy. The thing you are excited about is literally feeding you – but once it has passed, do you notice that same high level of energy, or are you returning to your usual reluctance to get up in the morning?

The same is true of our goals – when we are working toward something we want, we are focused and energized.

We all need something that excites us - a thing we would like to experience in our lives to give our days purpose and give us a reason to get up each morning.

The problem with a goal whose boundaries are always shifting is that we can easily become despondent as we work towards achieving our goal. We simply want to experience freedom from the grip of selective mutism, but no matter how many steps forward we seem to be taking, there are always more in front of us. Our goal is too big, too wide, too non-descript.

Just to add a little confusion into the mix, I do believe that it is important to have a larger vision for your life that doesn't have boundaries ... a way of being that you would like to keep on experiencing more of, for example. Inside of that vision is where you can set your goals. My life's vision is to 'freely express and experience my hopes and dreams'. It is expansive, elusive, and completely unattainable, in the sense that I don't think I will ever find that I have reached this goal and need to make a new one. My vision feeds me and gives my life purpose and meaning. As my hopes and dreams change and grow, my vision remains the same. However, if I didn't have some manageable goals to work toward within this vision, I would probably quickly become despondent and find that my life was lacking purpose and direction.

Whatever the big vision is in your life, it is important to keep it open-ended. If you don't already have a vision for your life, why not take a moment to think about it now? If you thought your vision was to be normal or to overcome selective mutism, see if you can think past this goal and imagine how you would like your life to feel if selective mutism was not a part of it. You then get to set some goals, which break your vision down into smaller steps that each feel attainable, measurable, and worthy of celebration on their own. Overcoming selective mutism might be one of these goals.

Next, break each goal down into three smaller steps, and then break each of these steps down until each one feels like it will be really easy for you to manage.

Suddenly, your overwhelming vision is made to feel much more simple because it is now a series of small steps that each feels attainable to you. It doesn't matter how small each one of these steps might seem to anybody else – the most important thing is that you feel that they are manageable. In my opinion, there is little more satisfying than being able to do something that you previously couldn't. It doesn't matter how small that thing may be, the feeling of satisfaction is completely valid.

What I'm saying here is that the more you break down your goals, the better. It's like pacing yourself when you set out to run a marathon – if you set out sprinting, you will very likely burn out quickly and probably will not finish. The same is true for achieving your larger goals and living each day with the passion and purpose that is fuelled by the unique vision that you have for your life.

22. Redefining 'Quiet'

There are so many wonderful qualities to be recognised ...

I f you look up the word 'quiet' in the dictionary, you will see a description that reads something along the lines of:

"Making or characterized by little or no noise.'

I never used to consider 'quiet' to be an accurate word to describe people like me. Of course, outwardly, anybody who suffers from selective mutism makes little or no noise, particularly in those situations that cause anxiety - but if you are anything like me, I'm sure you would agree that inside of our minds it is anything but quiet.

Inside the mind of a quiet person is a rich and interesting world full of thoughts and imaginings, observations and possibilities. Quiet has a depth to it that lends itself to exploration. It does not like to announce its presence, but it likes to be noticed all the same. The last thing Quiet wants is to be cast aside because of its unassuming nature.

Quiet is not a trait that typically receives celebration. Instead, us quiet folk are usually encouraged, coaxed, and pushed to participate before our sensitive systems have had time to adjust and process what we are being asked to do. We have our own pace, which we need to acknowledge and work with if we are to show our strengths and share our skills.

Quiet has a huge amount to offer, but it does not advertise this fact. Quiet gets on with things and sometimes wishes that others would see it for all that it is. Sometimes quiet feels anxious, shy, timid, or fearful, but in truth, quiet is none of these things.

The most empowering thing I think I have ever realized is the fact that I have a huge amount to offer exactly as I am. I do not need to change anything about myself, and I do not need to overcome anything to begin. If I look back upon my life, there is not one time when I can see myself as someone with nothing or little to offer, but for so long I thought I needed to reach a particular set

I HAVE SOMETHING TO SAY!

point before I could truly start living my life. It caused me a huge amount of additional anxiety as I constantly reached forward toward my ideal – an elusive goal that was always a little out of reach.

I do not need to shed any skin or overcome any of my quiet tendencies. It feels like such a relief to realize that I can live a useful and fulfilling life without changing one thing about my personality. I think the thing that caused me the most anxiety growing up was the idea that I would have to become someone else before I could live a worthwhile life. I thought that I needed to be more than I was, but this realization that quiet comes with its own set of gifts and qualities has helped me to fully embrace those that I carry.

Open, caring, helpful, creative, intelligent, thoughtful, imaginative, intuitive, meaningful, observant, capable, considerate, interesting … how many of these quiet traits can you identify with? How many more could you add to this list?

23. Being vulnerable

There is huge strength in declaring weakness ...

In 2012 I decided it was time to stand up and begin to talk about the various ways I had felt through my life. I wanted people to know about selective mutism, and I wanted to make sure that children who are suffering today wouldn't have to feel alone and misunderstood the way I once felt.

An opportunity to speak at a local TED-style event came up, and I volunteered to do it. At the same time, I decided that I would write a book, *this book*, and I began to prepare to share as much as I could about my life and the difficulties I had experienced surrounding selective mutism.

What I discovered, interestingly enough, was that speaking was one thing, but writing a book took my vulnerability to a whole new level. I knew I would have to get to know myself in a much deeper way than I had before. I would have to be prepared to explore my past and learn from it as much as I could if I wanted to achieve this goal. Writing this book has felt like something I've wanted and needed to do for a long time – in truth, I first decided I wanted to put my feelings into words when I was only six years old. I longed to be able to satisfy my desire to show people who I really am, instead of feeling like I was lost behind my silence and the behaviours that I genuinely couldn't control. I knew that when I eventually wrote this book I would be able to make peace with all of this, but the idea of actually doing it felt incredibly difficult.

I sat down to begin writing countless times, but every time I did I became overrun with fear. I was terrified because I knew that by writing this book, I would finally get to know myself in a way I had been too scared to before. I was scared that I would not like the person I discovered, and so I put it off until the pull to do it became so great I felt like I literally had no choice in the matter.

I realized that it takes a huge amount of strength to declare and acknowledge those parts of ourselves that we perceive to be our shortfalls, even to ourselves, but it is worth every yucky feeling we may encounter along the way.

It has only been through writing that I have begun

to discover the strengths and beauty that lay hidden behind my behavior – and this is what I want to share here.

To be vulnerable and to admit the ugliest parts of ourselves is to declare all that we are. To open up to our difficulties, our struggles, our challenges, our negative thoughts, our heavy emotions … every single perceived weakness takes strength to admit. I used to do my best to hide the parts of myself I perceived as my weaknesses, and I grew accustomed to glossing over my true feelings whilst claiming that everything was okay. However, when I began to admit the truth to myself, something magical happened.

The truth that I discovered was that within every dark corner of my being was a spark waiting to light it up. The power of vulnerability is the willingness to explore our shadows, and the hidden strengths and talents that we will find when we do. This is different to embodying our weaknesses – this is seeing those weaknesses for what they really are.

What are you really scared of? Who do you think you might discover if you start to explore your potential a little more deeply, a little more honestly? Are you more scared of the idea that you will fail or that you might finally become the person you have always dreamed of being?

Are you actually afraid of finding out that your excuses have been keeping you small? Are you scared to admit that you are only stuck living a life you don't like because of the choices you have made about what you will believe and accept for yourself? Do you feel like you've been living this way for so long that it's too late to change now?

I agree, it is a very difficult thing to be vulnerable, but admitting the truth of your life's circumstances may just be the most freeing, wonderful thing you will ever do for yourself.

24. Beyond selective mutism

This is who we are ...

For many years I had no idea that I had a lot to offer the world just by being myself. I thought I had to strive to be someone I wasn't, and to fit into this world the way it was already set up. I didn't realize that I was born with the potential to expand the world into something new. I had no idea that each of us has a part to play in creating our growing world as a place we love to live in. Much of my potential was hiding away, waiting for a simple acknowledgement to announce itself.

> *"I see you!"*
>
> *I look around, to check that no one else has noticed. It is scary enough acknowledging myself, let alone sharing this discovery with anyone else. It literally petrifies me to even imagine how it might feel to have someone else see me in this way – and yet it is this unconditional acceptance that I have craved for so long.*

*No expectations, no pressure, just a completely loving, accepting presence that knows without a doubt that **I am special, simply because I exist**. I don't need to talk, I don't need to smile, and I don't even need to show my face because I am already perfect exactly the way I am.*

With the release of the pressure and the knowledge that I can finally see, accept, and love myself exactly as I am, a huge weight is lifted from my shoulders. My anxiety eases with it, and I find that I appear to have more choices about the way I would like to live and present myself to the world.

I realise that I have been freed from my fear of the judgment of others. I begin to wonder how it would be to really talk to somebody new. I begin to experiment with sounds as I quietly hum my breath through my vocal chords.

This is my voice. These are my sounds. I am making them because I want to, and they feel good to me. If I had something to say, I would be able to say it too. That knowledge feels amazing. I can feel myself gaining in strength, and I tip my head up so that I can once again look into my eyes.

"I see you!"

Yes, I do – and I become aware of the tears, flowing freely across my cheeks and drip-dripping as they fall onto my hands. They are tears of relief, happy tears raining my fears and insecurities away.

My breathing is calm, and I smile at my reflection. I am free! I have not yet spoken, but I know now that there is no need to. I could, if I wanted to, but for the first time in years, there is nothing that I want to say. I simply want to stay here, in this moment, enveloped in the joy of this unfolding realization that I have nothing to prove and no one to please.

Selective mutism felt like a prison for years - and then, just like that, it was gone.

As I write it, I can feel the remnants of selective mutism lifting away from me. It no longer matters to me whether I can speak or whether I can't. People's opinions have become insignificant, and every single tension has dissolved in an instant. I understand that the potential for selective mutism remains, but it no longer has any hold on me. I feel strong in who I am, and excited for my future.

I am struck with the realisation that I have spent years aiming for an impossible goal. For most of my life I have been trying to overcome my own inherent nature. I have been trying to be someone I am not, trying to talk before I was ready, trying to share what was not yet ready to be spoken. I have been rushing myself just as society tried to rush me first, but now I have returned to the pace of my heart.

There is no rush here, for I know that all the words that I want to say will come when they are ready. I no longer feel anxious when I am asked a question and an answer does not leave my mouth in the following instant. I simply breathe a little and wait until my voice is ready. I sit inside of this place of calm, and I speak in my own time. The feeling of my words as they roll over my tongue and make their way into the world is like nothing else. These words were made to be spoken, but only when I feel ready to speak them. I am grateful that I kept going through every single tough time. I am thankful to be here, and I am delighted that I am finally able to see myself – perfect in this moment, whatever I choose.

The way I see it, you can let selective mutism define you, or you can **choose to define yourself** and be the sensitive, thoughtful, creative, intuitive, capable, intelligent, amazing person that you are – **regardless of whether you can talk or not.**

Epilogue

I decided that I would realize my six-year-old dream and write this book a few years ago, but as keen as I was to write it, I was scared. I knew that I would have to revisit aspects of myself that I had kept safely tucked away for many years – moving past behavior patterns that keep us stuck and unsatisfied in life can be hugely empowering, but it is also scary. If it was easy, they wouldn't be there, shaping our lives in ways that we would rather they didn't!

I found that the more I committed to wanting to write this book, the more I noticed parts of myself that were affected by anxiety. I began to see so many unconscious reactions that I had been turning a blind eye to for as long as I could remember, and I realised that selective mutism was still playing its part in my life. It was challenging to become much more aware of myself, and I became a little overwhelmed … but what I have found is that by writing about my observations, I was able to see them in a new light and appreciate what my behavior was trying to teach me.

Writing has been something that I consider a saving grace in my life. It has helped me to process my thoughts, feelings, and unexplainable behavior – so that I could begin to see them and myself in a new light. Writing this book has been an amazing thing to do because so much of my life and behavior now makes a lot more sense and affects me much less through my days, if at all. I can understand myself on a whole new level, and I also find that after writing about a particular issue it suddenly becomes less of a 'thing' for me. There is something hugely powerful about putting a problem into words. Maybe you find the same? I definitely recommend writing in some context as a way to process difficult feelings and then move past them.

In my late twenties, writing involved journaling and hashing out my feelings with strong, harsh marks on paper. The strength of my emotions would literally rip through pages ... but it helped me tremendously! If you are not a writing person, I encourage you to find a similar medium that works for you. Perhaps it is art, music, movement ... whatever it is, the ability to safely navigate old feelings and beliefs that are preventing you from moving forward with your life has the capacity to completely transform your experience.

We all have our own path to follow, and what worked for me might not work for you, but regardless of what you take away from this book, I hope that my words have been able to help you to feel a little more compassionate toward yourself, a little more understanding of your least favourite parts, and a little more willing or optimistic about your future. (Or those of your child, student, friend, or whomever else this might apply to!) Most of all, I wish you love, luck, understanding, and acceptance on your own personal journey!

Acknowledgments

First and foremost, I do not think I would have gotten anywhere without the support of Simon Rasmussen, my partner for the past thirteen years and father of my children. Simon has understood very little about my struggles, but regardless, he has stood beside me – always believing that one day I might shoot out the other side, and for this belief alone, I owe the creation of this book.

To my children, Ashley and Cole, who continue to teach me more each day than I ever thought there was to learn. I definitely wouldn't have got this far without you both and the beautiful brightness you bring into my life.

Mum and Dad, you have always been there, even if I didn't recognize it at the time ... thank you for all you have done and continue to do to support me in living the life I choose.

Offering friendship, belief, clarity, direction, support, encouragement, perspective, and love, I thank the hundreds of people who have also impacted my life and played their own part in creating this book. There are too many to name, but I'd like to share a massive amount of gratitude to you all – writing this book has been a huge milestone in my life. xx

About the author

Kathryn Harper lives in Wanaka, New Zealand with her partner Simon and their two children, Ashley and Cole. She works part-time as an author-illustrator and has created the 'Katie-Jane series' to help children to understand emotional concepts and make sense of their difficult feelings. Kathryn also writes about selective mutism and anxiety on her blog at **kathrynharper.net**.

Selective Mutism Awareness New Zealand

Voice is a brand new charity working in New Zealand toward selective mutism awareness, understanding, and effective treatment.

It is our belief that through early recognition and effective treatment, selective mutism symptoms become less acute and often disappear altogether. We think it is hugely important to educate all adults who have an impact in children's lives of the tell-tale signs of selective mutism and the most effective ways to work with the underlying anxiety.

Please visit our website to learn more:

www.selectivemutism.org.nz

By purchasing this book you are supporting the work of Voice in spreading awareness and resources about selective mutism in New Zealand.